The (Reluctant, Nervous, Lazy, Broke, Busy, Confused) College Student's COOKBOOK

Acknowledgments

Without the help of many people, this book still may have been written; it just would have been a lot less, well, good.

Adam Weisman helped me out by designing some key recipes and providing a lot of basic culinary information. David Silver and Rachel Jacobson lent their not-insignificant knowledge of how to get by in the kitchen, along with a lot of "hands-on" help. Aaron Izenberg demonstrated a love of food not easily matched. Dan Bress came through with advice on being cheap. Steve Jeppson-Gamez, as usual, wisely counseled me on the subject he knows best. Danny Chun and Liz Phong gave tips on serving big groups. The ten interns at SPS Studios were also there from beginning to end with authentic and useful suggestions. Two no-longer-college-students, Allie and Joel Green, also chipped in with a few excellent recipes.

Two generous professional nutritionists helped me with all manner of questions on nutritional content. My wonderful sister, Sarah Lambert, gave me open access to her extensive knowledge. Barbara Boothby gave me a second look at some helpful hints that the Harvard University Health Services nutritionists published for the students there.

Two more women need to be thanked, not just for the extensive editing help they gave me with this book and for the recipes they contributed, but also for feeding me so well for twenty-one years of my life. They are, of course, my grandmother, Bess Kirsh, and my mother, Elaine Lambert. These amazing women gave me an appreciation for food that was instrumental in putting this book together.

And, of course, Stephen and Susan Polis Schutz and everyone at SPS Studios who encouraged this half-baked idea from the moment I cooked it up and who saw it through until the end.

Thanks!

Joshua N. Lambert

The *(Reluctant, Nervous, Lazy, Broke, Busy, Confused)* College Student's COOKBOOK

Joshua N. Lambert

Illustrated by Debby Lee

Blue Mountain Press™

SPS Studios, Inc., Boulder, Colorado

Library of Congress Catalog Card Number: 2001001966
ISBN: 0-88396-591-7

Manufactured in China
First Printing: June 2001

 This book is printed on recycled paper.

This book is printed on fine quality, laid embossed, 80 lb. paper. This paper has been specially produced to be acid free (neutral pH) and contains no groundwood or unbleached pulp. It conforms with all the requirements of the American National Standards Institute, Inc., so as to ensure that this book will last and be enjoyed by future generations.

Library of Congress Cataloging-in-Publication Data

Lambert, Joshua N.
The (reluctant, nervous, lazy, broke, busy, confused) college student's cookbook / Joshua N. Lambert ; illustrated by Debby Lee.
p. cm.
Includes index.
ISBN 0-88396-591-7 (softcover : alk. paper)
1. Cookery. I. Title.
TX652 .L238 2001
641.5—dc21

2001001966
CIP

SPS Studios, Inc.
P.O. Box 4549, Boulder, Colorado 80306

Contents

Introduction

Don't be afraid. Yes, this is a cookbook. And yes, it is *your* cookbook now.

We know; it's pretty scary. You're thinking that cooking your own food is going to be hard, annoying, frustrating, time consuming — and to top it all off, if you mess it up, you'll be hospitalized for either food poisioning or starvation. Sure, you *probably* won't starve to death if you don't learn to cook for yourself — there are lots of restaurants around that you can eat at. But if you *do* use this book to learn how to cook, you'll soon have more money, more time, more friends, more energy, and more confidence. You'll be healthier next week and sixty years from now. You'll probably win a Nobel Prize or an Olympic medal or something.

This book is divided into three major sections. In the first — "Before You Cook" — you'll learn about those scary metal things in your kitchen. You'll learn how to shop like a pro, and you'll learn what to do in order to avoid poisoning yourself. You should read this section start to finish and follow its instructions before you start to cook.

In the second section — "Now Cook!" — you'll learn how to prepare food for every conceivable situation in your life, from waking up for a 4:30 a.m. fire drill to asking your parents for more money. You should use this section as you need it; just turn to the chapter that applies to your current predicament. For instance, if thirty-five people show up at your door demanding food, you should flip to "'Anybody got a Hairnet?': Cooking for a Crowd." If it's 7:00 on Tuesday night and you're starving, open to "The Fundamentals: How to Make Dinner 76 Nights in a Row."

In the third section — "Oh, So You're Done Cooking, Are You?" — you'll get some extra help with the cooking process. You'll find a Recipe Index that will help you find the meal you want to make right now. You'll also find a section called "Further Research," in which you can find out how to learn even more about cooking than this book could ever tell you.

But that's a long way off. For now, walk over to your kitchen. Take a deep breath. Believe it or not, you're about to become a cook. Feeling relaxed? Ready to go?

Good. Turn to "The Sixty-Minute Kitchen Set-Up" and let's get cooking.

The Sixty-Minute Kitchen Set-Up

All of a sudden you've got your own kitchen. All those shiny steel instruments and polished surfaces — which were so harmless and even cute in your parents' kitchen — are now dangerous and mysterious tools of potential self-mutilation. Not to fear. A kitchen, like a dog, is easy to manage, so long as you keep it on a short leash and always clean up the mess. Your first task is to familiarize yourself with the utilities and tools in your kitchen, their functions, and how to use them most effectively to make the food you want in the time you have. There are really only seven basic kinds of kitchen appliances:

Things to Keep Stuff Cold:

You may be familiar with the most common items in this category: the fridge and freezer. Other entries include the mini-fridge, portable cooler, and automatic icemaker. You need these things to keep perishable food, like meat and cheese, from spoiling over long periods of time — as well as to keep your ice cream from melting and to make your drinks cold. As a category, these aren't absolutely necessary (see medieval history and beef jerky), but if you'd prefer to avoid scurvy and the stench of rotting meat, make sure you have at least one cold-making device on hand. Before using it, take five minutes to make sure it's clean and empty of unidentified biological substances.

Things to Make Stuff Hot:

The main difference, in terms of food preparation, between human society and the animal kingdom is... fire. Of the devices that will help you raise your meals to an appetizing temperature, there are three sub-categories: "Things That Heat Surfaces," "Things That Heat the Entire Solid Piece of Food," and "Things That Heat Liquid."

Surface-heating devices include hot plates, electric griddles, barbecue grills, and the traditional combination of a stovetop with a frying pan. Basically, all you need is a source of heat (in its most basic form: fire) and a flat, heat-conducting surface (a metal plate). These devices are used for all sorts and variations of frying.

"Things That Heat the Entire Solid Piece of Food" are better known as ovens. They range in size from toaster ovens to those huge wood-burning pizza ovens you see at trendy Italian restaurants. Microwaves do the job of an oven quickly and efficiently. **(Note: Don't put any metal objects into a microwave oven.)**

Heating liquid is easy. Just put the liquid in a container (heat-conducive like metal is best) and then apply heat through any number of sources. An immersion heater, an electric kettle, a stovetop, or a small fire on the floor of your apartment will work fine, though the latter might create some difficulty at clean-up time.

Microwaves and other ovens can also be used to boil water, though of course you can't stir or add ingredients to the boiling mixture.

Here's a quick explanation of a few words you will see often in the recipes in this book, as well as in other cookbooks, when you are asked to fry, warm, or boil stuff.

Low heat: About as low as the knob that controls temperature on the stovetop goes. If you were putting something in the oven, this is equal to about 250° Fahrenheit, which is about 120° Celsius.
Medium-low heat: Turn the knob a little higher than low heat. Oven-wise, it should be about 300° Fahrenheit, which is about 150° Celsius.
Medium heat: Halfway between the lowest and the highest setting on your stovetop. The equivalent oven temperature is about 350° Fahrenheit, which is about 175° Celsius.
Medium-high heat: A little higher than medium heat, which is equal to an oven temperature of about 400° Fahrenheit, or 205° Celsius.
High heat: As close to high as your stovetop will go. Your oven can probably get up to about 450° Fahrenheit, which is about 230° Celsius.

If you don't have at least one appliance in each of the above categories, make a mental note. When you get to the end of this chapter, run to the nearest kitchen-supply store or big department store to buy yourself the cheapest toaster oven, disposable barbecue, or electric kettle they have. Most of these appliances should be available for less than fifty bucks. Once you've got all these appliances, take a few minutes to turn each one on and off and fiddle with the dials for adjusting temperature until you feel comfortable operating them.

Things That Cut Stuff Up:

Cutting is a crucial part of the food preparation process; if it weren't for cutting, you'd have to eat an entire cow every time you wanted a hamburger. So you're going to need a sharp instrument — a cutting knife, a clean pair of scissors, or an 18th century guillotine. And though there are thousands of knives, slicers, dicers, and graters on the market, there's not a whole lot you can't do with one good knife and some strong wrist action. One of the few things you definitely *cannot* do is blend food into a watery pulp or crush ice effectively, so you may want to think about purchasing a blender if you plan to make any kind of smoothie, shake, or several kinds of sauces.

Things That Put Food into Your Mouth:

Once you've got food to eat, you're going to need to get it into your mouth. Your hands are natural silverware, of course, but a little *actual* silverware may come in handy if you make, for instance, soup. The important thing to remember when evaluating your silverware situation is that people are always giving away free plastic silverware, so if you hang out in a food court with your eyes open long enough, you'll probably find a willing benefactor. You should also remember that forks, knives, plates, and cups are only one mode of social food intake; some people use chopsticks to eat everything from steak to rice — and who among us is too good for an old-fashioned food trough?

Things That Are Comprised of Two Hydrogen Atoms and One Oxygen Atom:

Water. You need lots of it. Running water is probably best — certainly better than a well or a truckload of bottled water — and if you can combine good, clean running water with a drainable tub, you've got yourself a sink. Even the most down-to-earth (i.e., cheap) cook should be fastidiously clean — that is, unless you like bacterial infections. Keeping your cooking areas and hands clean will make your food taste better and less like dirt.

Things That Measure Food:

To follow recipes in this book or any other, you're going to need to know how much a teaspoon is, as well as about a dozen other cooking-specific measurements. We'll try to simplify them for you, and if you don't have a measuring cup, we'll give you directions on how to make your own in about five minutes.

For teaspoons and tablespoons, it helps to have at least a couple standard pieces of silverware. Teaspoons are the little ones and tablespoons are the big ones; some people call tablespoons soup spoons. Teaspoons hold about 5 ml, and tablespoons about 15 ml. In terms of measuring for recipes, you can buy a cheap set of measuring spoons or you can just approximate with the spoons you use to eat with. You can also estimate with bottle caps: a big, deep bottle cap that you might find on a bottle of vodka is probably going to be equal to a tablespoon, while a shallow, small bottle cap that you might find on a bottle of mineral water is probably equal to just a little more than a teaspoon. For some reason, someone, somewhere set a standard cup size, even though we're sure the cups in your kitchen are anything but standard. A cup, when we're talking about cooking, is equal to 250 ml.

To make your own measuring cup:

1. Get yourself a one-liter bottle of soda.
2. Drink the soda.
3. Fill the bottle almost to the top with water.
4. Get four cups or glasses, preferably the kind that you can see through. Line them up in a row. Pour the water into the four glasses so that there's the same amount in each.

5. Pick a different glass or cup, the biggest one you've got, to be your measuring cup forever. (You can even cut the spout off the top of the original soda bottle and use that, if it's transparent.) Stick a piece of transparent tape on the outside, running from top to bottom.
6. Pour the water from one of your cups into your measuring cup. Use a black marker to mark the water level on the tape. This is 250 ml, which is approximately one cup.
7. Pour in the water from one of the other cups. Mark the water level — this is 500 ml, or two cups.
8. Do it again with the other two cups, and now you have a measuring cup of up to four cups.

For other measuring information, like converting between metric and imperial measurement systems and dealing with things like quarts and pints and deciliters and other weird stuff, see the conversion table at the back of this book.

Three Semi-Important Things That Don't Easily Fit into the Categories Above:

There are many purpose-specific tools that will make your life in the kitchen much, much easier. Of these, there are three that we think are important enough to mention: a spatula, a strainer, and a can opener. A spatula will allow you to lift and move the things you'll be frying in your frying pan. A strainer (also called a colander when it's bigger and has a base) will allow you to separate food from water, and will also let you steam vegetables. If you ever want to eat something that comes out of a can — like tuna, beans, or corn — you'll also need either a can opener or very sharp teeth. Each of these items should cost no more than a couple bucks and is available at most supermarkets, hardware stores, and kitchen-supply stores.

This is the most basic, pared-down description of a kitchen that we could get away with. If you don't have at least one object that approximates each of the categories above, you might be standing in an elevator, not a kitchen. The only other thing you're going to need in your kitchen is somewhere to put the food. If your kitchen doesn't come with enough cabinet space, consider dedicating a nearby bookshelf or a free-standing closet to hold your food; it'll make it easier for you to organize and find what you're looking for.

Speaking of food, you're going to need some. And not just a little. In the next chapter, you're going shopping — and this is probably the most difficult, most important part of cooking.

The Fifteen-Minute, Twice-a-Month Shopping Plan

Shopping effectively can make the difference between enjoying your time in the kitchen and hating it more than you hate that guy who always sits in the front row in chemistry lecture. Just imagine being the perfect shopper — every time you need something, it's right there in front of you, just waiting to be used. You never run out of the things you like best, and you never have to worry about getting midway through a recipe and not being able to finish. Not only that, but you never have to go out to the market to buy something special for that day's dinner — you've already got it.

Shopping like this is possible... *if* you understand your ingredients and the way you store and eat them.

For the purpose of this book, there are three types of ingredients. The first type are *stock ingredients*: those that you can keep in your fridge or pantry (i.e., a cupboard or basically anywhere) for long periods of time, and which you should have a stock of at all times. You'll need to buy a lot of stock items on your first trip to the store, and after that you'll probably want to update only once a month or less. The second type are *fresh ingredients*: those that spoil readily, need to be kept in the fridge or freezer, and will be the bulk of what you buy on your bi-monthly shopping excursions. Examples are milk, bread, cheese, and meat. The third type are *luxury ingredients*: these are the ones that don't really fit into a student's budget. You certainly can use these as much as you care to or can afford to, but they'll be included as options in the recipes so that they can be used when your cash flow is high and disregarded when your phone bill is due.

This chapter, then, will be split into three parts: how to buy stock items, how to buy fresh items, and a general section on how to shop effectively.

Stock Items

The stock items in your fridge and pantry will form the backbone of your kitchen. If you buy successfully, you'll be able to survive gastronomically on these items alone, though you probably won't enjoy doing so. More important, though, will be your ability to complement your fresh items and create interesting and original menus.

The table below is included for your convenience while shopping for stock items, starting with your very first time. The items near the top of the list take a while to spoil (at least a month and usually many months, if stored properly), but will go bad eventually. We're not going to advise you to take any significant chances with your health and well-being; if you'd like to play Russian roulette with a thirteen-month-old banana, that's your prerogative.

The truth is that most items on the list should store almost indefinitely as far as you're concerned because you'll finish them long before they spoil. So you should feel free to buy as much of these as you can (without filling up your living room with canned peaches and boxes of garbage bags). In reality, the limiting factor on how much you buy of just about any of these ingredients is going to be how much you can carry. The per-month suggested quantity is there to make sure you don't buy too little. By all means, buy much more than that if you can get it back to your place and have somewhere to put it. Specifically, with honey and mustard and other condiments that are sold both in tiny, high-priced bottles and in big, bargain containers, buy the big one. For that first-time shopping trip, you should definitely either take a cab home from the supermarket or borrow a car if you don't have one.

Also note that the quantities suggested here are for just one person who entertains once or twice a week, not for the entire volleyball team. So don't be surprised if food starts disappearing quickly when your neighbors start figuring out that you have a lot of it. Get a lock on your door. And of course, buy more of what you like and less of what you don't. We shouldn't have to tell you that.

One more thing: the "Storage Location" column might be confusing if you don't know what a *pantry* is. That's just a shelf or closet where you keep food. It's warmer and lighter than *a cool, dark place*.

Ingredient	**Per-Month Suggested Qty.**	**Storage Location**
Potatoes (in a big canvas sack)	15 medium potatoes	a cool, dark place
Garlic	4 bulbs	pantry
Onions	15 small onions	a cool, dark place
Rice	750 grams	pantry

Dried pasta (any kind you like — spirals, if you don't know what else to get)	750 grams	pantry
Breakfast cereal/granola (in sealed bags)	1 kilogram	pantry
Crackers (in sealed bags)	A couple hundred crackers (about half a kilogram's worth)	pantry
Canned tuna	8 6-oz cans	pantry
Canned tomatoes	2 16-oz cans	pantry
Canned fruit	5 cans	pantry
Canned corn	5 cans	pantry
Brown sugar	¼ pound	pantry
Sugar	¼ pound	pantry
Salt and pepper	¼ pound each	pantry
Baking soda	Very little — one package should keep you for the whole year	fridge
Baking powder	Very little — same as baking soda	pantry
Cooking/corn/vegetable oil	½ liter	pantry
Olive oil	½ liter	pantry
Peanut butter	1 large jar	pantry
Honey	250 ml	pantry
Balsamic vinegar	½ liter	pantry
Coffee	1 small jar	pantry
Tea	20 teabags	pantry
Garbage bags	4 bags	Who cares?
Dish soap	1/3 bottle (i.e., one bottle every three months)	by the sink
Cooking/cheap wine (optional)	1 bottle	pantry (if it's white, throw it in the fridge a couple hours before using)
Barbecue sauce	250 ml	fridge
Ketchup	250 ml	fridge
Mustard	250 ml	fridge
Soy sauce	250 ml	pantry

Canned juice	12 cans (if you have the freezer space for them)	freezer
Olives	1 small jar	fridge
Pickles	1 small jar	fridge
Salsa	500 ml	fridge (once opened)
Nuts	1 small jar	pantry
Nacho chips/taco shells (sealed)	1 big bag of chips or 6 shells	pantry
Tortillas (sealed)	6 tortillas	pantry
Flour	¼ pound	pantry
Dried chicken/beef stock/bouillon	1 liter	pantry
Soft drinks	24 cans	pantry (put them in the fridge before you drink them)

Dried Herbs and Spices

Dried herbs and spices keep almost forever, too. These are essential in flavoring your food. You should try as many as you can and get to know which you like and which you hate. Then when you're cooking, use the ones you like instead of the ones you hate. For buying them, the best place you can go is to a dollar store. These stores are full of all kinds of weird junk that only costs a dollar. Often, they'll also have reasonably large bottles of dried herbs and spices that cost — you guessed it — only a dollar. If you can't find a dollar store in your town, you can also find all of these at your regular or bulk supermarket, and they still won't be too expensive. There are plenty of fun and impractical spices that go beyond what would be used in a professional kitchen. You can buy rainbow sprinkles and "soul spice" and a list of other out-there spices.

Name	What it does
Cayenne pepper	Makes food spicy
Chili powder (should be stored in the fridge)	Makes food spicy
Onion powder	Makes food oniony
Garlic powder	Makes food garlicky
Dill	Strong, tangy flavor
Savory	Is not just an adjective, but a spice with a pine scent and a peppery flavor

Ginger	Slightly sweet, mint-like taste
Cinnamon	Sweet, spicy taste — good in hot drinks and desserts, and also with lamb
Basil	Nutty herb — great with pasta and with tomatoes
Oregano	Peppery but not too spicy — classic with tomato sauce and on pizza
Parsley	Neutral, fresh tasting
Cilantro/coriander	Even lighter flavor than parsley
Rosemary	Strong herb, good with potatoes
Chives	Neutral herb — use in salads
Mint	You should know what this tastes like
Curry	Sort of hot, but with its own distinctive flavor — if you've ever had Indian food before, it tastes like that
Paprika (should be stored in the fridge)	The ubiquitous Hungarian spice; it goes in everything and gives it a little tangy taste
Tarragon	Tastes a little like black licorice — often used with lamb

Fresh Items

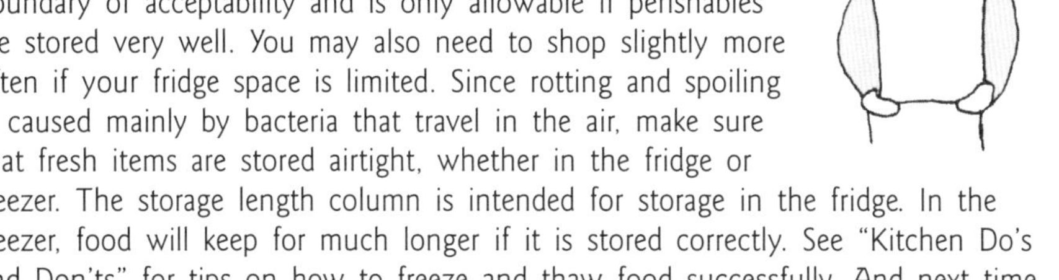

Unlike the stock items in the previous table, this one lists minimum storage in increments of two weeks. In some cases, keeping fresh items for two weeks might be just pushing the boundary of acceptability and is only allowable if perishables are stored very well. You may also need to shop slightly more often if your fridge space is limited. Since rotting and spoiling is caused mainly by bacteria that travel in the air, make sure that fresh items are stored airtight, whether in the fridge or freezer. The storage length column is intended for storage in the fridge. In the freezer, food will keep for much longer if it is stored correctly. See "Kitchen Do's and Don'ts" for tips on how to freeze and thaw food successfully. And next time you're out shopping, pick up some plastic airtight containers to use for storing leftovers.

And by all means, don't wait two weeks just because we tell you to. If there's a supermarket or grocery store convenient to you, you might as well stop there more often so that you won't have to eat dried-out bread. But from experience, we know that in reality it may often be two weeks between your shopping trips, so we've tried to suggest quantities that fit that time period. Again, don't take chances with food that doesn't smell right, look right, or taste right near the end of the two-week period.

Ingredient	Per 2-Week Suggested Qty.	Maximum Storage Time (Fridge)
Milk	4 liters	See expiration date
Butter or margarine	125 grams	Two months
Cheese	300 grams	In an unopened package, two months, depending on expiration date on package — once opened, at least two weeks, if wrapped well after each use
Yogurt	12 ounces	See expiration date
Eggs	1 dozen	Two weeks
Bread	3 large loaves	Keep one loaf in the fridge and the rest in the freezer to be thawed later — for the loaf in the fridge, you should have about five days before it gets moldy, if you reseal it faithfully
Pita	15	Same as bread
Fresh juice	1 liter	About a week in the fridge
Ground beef/chicken/pork/lamb	2 pounds, in smaller bags if possible	A day or two, depending on how fresh it was when you bought it — ask at the store
Chicken breasts/chicken thighs/beef steak filets/pork chops/fish filets/other cuts of meat	5	A day or two, depending on how fresh it was when you bought it — ask at the store
Tomatoes	10	About a week
Lettuce	2 heads	Four days (always tear leaves with your hands; never cut with a knife, or the edges will turn brown)
Cucumbers	3	One week
Mushrooms	1 small package	Four days
Red/green peppers	7	One week — but only a couple days after you cut into them
Fresh corn (in season in the summer, so this doesn't really apply to you during the school year)	2 ears	Three days
Bananas	4	Store them out in the open — they're ripe when they're yellow, and after that, three to five days

Sour cream	1 small container	About a week and a half; check expiration date
Berries	1 small container	Four days
Apples	4	Two weeks
Oranges	4	Two weeks
Cream cheese	100 grams	Probably a few weeks; check expiration date

How to Shop... Cheaply:

To pay less for groceries, the most important factor is to find a store that doesn't charge a lot. For bulk quantities (i.e., your stock items), a warehouse store is your best bet to get the most food for your buck. Small neighborhood markets and convenience stores will very likely do their best to rip you off. A general rule is that the bigger the store is, the cheaper the food will be.

Once you've found a reasonable store, buy the larger size of items to get slightly better per-unit costs. Always remember to do your math when buying in quantity. Many supermarkets have taken to listing the unit cost of their products, but if they don't, you should always calculate how much you're paying per gram, ounce, or item when buying more than a little.

Also, be aware of sources of extra-cheap or free food items — and this doesn't just mean mooching off your parents or charging groceries to their credit cards — but also availing yourself of free condiments at restaurants and low-cost produce at farmer's markets, especially around closing time. See page 83 for many more hints on eating on a wafer-thin budget.

How to Shop... Within a Budget:

Shopping for food is expensive, almost always more expensive than you think it will be. The best way to shop without blowing your budget is to go into the store with reasonable expectations of what you will spend. Try to calculate what you would spend eating at a nearby restaurant for three meals a day plus snacks for the two-week or month-long period you're shopping for. Then divide that number in half or even quarters and you'll have a reasonably approximate figure for what you should expect to spend in a supermarket. If you're shopping and the prices seem too high or your bill seems to add up too quickly, compare the prices per item to what you would pay at a restaurant. If you're paying a good amount less (at least 35%) than you would have to pay someone else to do all the work, then you're fine. If you're paying more, run — and find a different store. Students we know have said that they've been able to get by quite well on $35-45 a week.

How to Shop... Quickly:

To make your rounds of the supermarket as quick as possible, create a shopping list that corresponds to the location of the food. The lists given above are cross-checked against the layout strategies of a couple large American supermarkets, but you should certainly monkey with them according to the peculiarities of your market. Rather than writing up a new list every two weeks, save yourself time by creating a table like the one shown previously, either by hand or on a word processing program. Then make a bunch of photocopies of it before adding in the required quantities and rushing off to the store. Then you can zip through your kitchen for two minutes before you leave for the store, fill in the necessary quantities on one of your premade shopping lists, and blitz through the market in a matter of just a few more minutes.

Kitchen Do's and Don'ts

Now, if you've been following this book's instructions like a good kid, you should have a kitchen with some food in it. You're all set to whip up some foie gras sautéed with fresh cilantro and celeriac, right?

Hold up a sec. There are a *lot* of things you might not know yet about this business called cooking, and you might want to cruise through our exhaustive list of kitchen tips below before you dive headfirst into your first stir-fry. They'll probably save you more than a couple times from embarrassing — or worse, endangering and nauseating — yourself. The tips are organized in loose categories, so you can come back to them before you start any process that you feel a little shaky about. But the most important thing is to get into the kitchen and make your own mistakes. Before you know it, you'll be adding your own tips to the lists below.

Cleanliness

Even if you break every other rule that this book gives you, it would truly be in your best interest to pay close attention to these cleanliness tips. Otherwise, you may well find yourself becoming much more intimate with the toilet and possibly hospitalized.

- That patch of white, green, or other unusually colored gunk on your aging bread or cheese is mold. Don't eat it — it's bacteria. On the other hand, don't be afraid of it. Especially with cheese, you can cut off the moldy part and eat the rest.

- If you can, wash dishes, pots, and pans soon after you use them. You shouldn't put a boiling hot pot or pan in cold water because it'll warp the shape, but as soon as the pan is cool, start scrubbing. It'll be easier to get the food off than if you let it harden for a couple weeks.

- Don't scrimp on soap, and don't get lazy with the caked-on pieces on your plates and pots. Eating good food on dirty dishes is like watching *The Godfather* on a Gameboy.

- Remember to wash your dishtowels — say, once a week with your bed sheets. If you're not washing your bed sheets that often, well... you should.

- While you're cooking, don't be afraid to get your hands dirty, and don't be afraid to wash them over and over again. Dirty — clean — dirty — clean — dirty — clean — it's a rough life, to be a cook's hand.

- When we say "wash," we mean with soap and hot water. Don't think that rinsing alone is going to kill stomach-turning bacteria.

- If you're just cooking for yourself and the last time you cleaned the floor of your kitchen was in recorded history, then the five-second rule can apply if you want it to: if a dropped piece of food has been on the ground for less than five seconds, it's still edible.

- You may need to lay bottles of liquid flat on one of the shelves in your fridge in order to fit them in. If so, make sure the caps are on really tight or everything in your fridge will soon be covered in mango-guava juice.

- Uncooked meat can kill you. Be very careful with it. Anything that has been used to cut, touch, hold, or has otherwise come in contact with raw meat needs to be washed before it touches anything else. This includes your hands, dishtowels, knives, forks, plates, cutting boards, and countertops. Store raw meat in separate, tightly wrapped containers in the fridge or freezer so that gross raw meat juices don't seep down into your clean food.

Freezing/Refrigerating

- If you need lots of ice cubes and don't have enough ice trays to satisfy your need, try making ice and then bagging it or just leaving it in a bowl in the freezer. Then make more in the trays and keep saving it.

- If you don't periodically (once a month) clear out the frost that may build up around the edges of your freezer compartment, you may soon find yourself with a freezer that looks like an igloo. You'll lose valuable space in there, and it's much tougher to get that weird frost out when a lot of it has built up.

- It's not so good to thaw frozen foods on the countertop. When you need to thaw food, it's much better to leave it in the fridge (where thawing will take longer but be safer), hold it under lukewarm water in a sealed plastic bag, or put it in the microwave.

- You should refrigerate food quickly. Leaving leftovers on the counter for more than two hours may allow them to spoil. Wrap them up and get them in the fridge.

- You can thaw raw meat only once, so don't thaw more meat than you're going to use. If you do end up thawing too much meat, cook all of it and store it in the fridge or freeze it again cooked, rather than refreezing the raw stuff.

- Smaller containers get colder quicker, so if you have a lot of leftovers to store, it's better to divide them into several small containers than put them in one mammoth one.

- If you freeze something and it's not sealed well, it'll get freezer burn. This is a layer of weird frost on top of the food. It won't hurt you, but it will make the food less palatable. It's not the end of the world if it happens, but you should make sure that you freeze things in sturdy, airtight containers or that you meticulously plastic-wrap them.

Boiling

- If you're boiling water for pasta and leave the temperature too high after you've put the pasta in, the pot will boil over and spill all over your stove. Don't do that.

- If you're trying to get water to a boil, cover the top of the pot with its lid or with a plate. That traps the heat inside and speeds up the process. But if you leave the lid on when you have pasta inside the hot water, it'll boil over.

- Dissolved salts and things in water raise its boiling point. (Remember eleventh grade chemistry?) So, the cleaner the pot, the quicker it'll boil.

- If possible, stir pasta in boiling water with a wooden spoon or other blunt, non-conductive object, like a hockey stick. You won't scratch the bottom of the pot, and the wood won't conduct heat and burn your hand.

- In general, toss a little salt in a pot of boiling water before you add the food to it. In particular, make sure you add salt when you're hard-boiling an egg; it'll ensure that if the shell somehow cracks, the egg won't run all over the pan.

Grilling/Frying/Roasting/Microwaving/Barbecuing

- When heating a liquid in a bowl in the microwave, you can cover it with plastic wrap to seal in the heat, but make sure you poke a good number of holes in the plastic wrap for the air to escape through. Otherwise, the heat will build up inside the bowl and then explode, splattering the inside of your microwave worse than a Jackson Pollock painting.

- When you put a pan for frying on the stove, put a pat of butter on it right away. As the pan heats up, the butter will melt and when it's all melted away, you'll know the pan is hot enough to fry.

- When barbecuing, it might seem like a good idea to build a really big fire and let the fire touch the meat to cook it faster. That's fine, but you'll cover your meat in that black stuff (ash) — though some people like that kind of taste.

- This tip is particularly important. You've got to cook your meat thoroughly or it can be dangerous. (See the previous bit on raw meat.) If possible, get an internal thermometer that you can shove into the meat to know that it's hot enough. You'll be fine if all your meat is at least 160° Fahrenheit and at least 180° for chicken and turkey.

- Fish should be cooked until you can flake it with a fork — that means that when you press down on it, little chunks flake off easily.

- It's also important to cook your eggs thoroughly. Raw eggs sometimes have bacteria that can hurt you. See the section on eggs in "The Fundamentals," page 44, for more information on how you should approach raw eggs.

- Food shrinks when you cook it. A piece of raw chicken, for instance, will shrink to about three-quarters the size after it's cooked. Keep this in mind when you're deciding how much of something to make; it's a good rule to always make a little more than you think you'll need. One of your mooch neighbors will be happy to take the extra off your hands, or you can save the leftovers for later.

- Microwaves don't like metal. Don't put anything with metal in a microwave or it'll catch fire. This includes aluminum foil, gold-rimmed plates (we're sure you have lots of those), and twist-ties with aluminum wires in them.

Cutting/Blending

- Always use a cutting board or you'll tear up your countertops.

- If you have a good, strong knife with a sharp blade, you can chop up vegetables the way chefs do. Put the tip of the blade down on the cutting board and keep it there by pressing down on it with the heel of one hand. Then lift the back of the knife up and down with the other hand, always keeping the tip touching the board. Chopping goes really quick that way.

- If you want to press garlic and don't have a garlic press — and you probably don't — just peel the skin off the garlic, chop it up, and then use the flat side of your knife to press the pieces into a paste. Alternate chopping and pressing until you get it as thick as you want it.

- Don't ever cut something with the blade facing toward your hand. Or your face, for that matter.

- If you're passing a knife to somebody, pass it handle-first, carefully.

- If you're cutting soft cheese, you can slice it with a dull butter knife and get good, thin slices.

- If your blender seems to be stuck, try changing the speeds or turning it off and shaking the mixture up.

- Don't crush ice in a blender that doesn't specifically have an ice-crushing function. Or, wait — you can, but know that if you do, you'll probably ruin it much more quickly than you otherwise would have. To prolong blender life in this situation, put your ice in a plastic bag and step on it, hit it with a hammer, throw it at the wall, or otherwise manually crush it before you blend it.

Ingredients and Recipes

- All recipes, not just the ones in this book, are meant to guide you without forcing you to do anything. If you just follow instructions, you'll never really understand what you're doing. Branch out, try new things, experiment. It'll pay off in the long run, even if you mess up one meal.

- Go nuts with salt, pepper, and other spices. Though salt has some negative health effects, pepper and other spices are not particularly bad for you and you can add as much as you like. We'll try to remind you of this throughout the recipes, but you should *always* add salt, pepper, herbs, and spices to taste. (Well, not to ice cream, but in all other cases.)

- Add fresh herbs at the end of preparing your recipe. They're so full of flavor that cooking them won't do much to help. If you're using dried herbs, though, you'll probably want to add them as soon as possible. Heating them will help the flavor spread throughout the food.

- Substitutions are often possible. In making pancakes or scrambled eggs, for instance, if you're out of milk, you can substitute water. They won't be as fluffy and nice as if you used milk, but it won't particularly ruin the recipe.

- Always preheat your oven before cooking. Turn it on to the desired temperature ten minutes before you're ready to put the food in — the little light should go off when the oven is up to your desired temperature.

- You should use the middle of your oven unless told to do otherwise (and you won't be told to do otherwise in this book). The top part of the oven should be the hottest, and the bottom should be the coolest (because heat rises, you humanities majors). But the heat comes out from the bottom, so that part might be hotter. Bottom line: put stuff in the middle, and don't worry about it.

- You're mostly going to have to figure out cooking times for yourself. The times in this book, and in any recipe you get, are approximate. With most foods, you can check periodically to see if they're ready, either by taking a bite (with pasta, rice, or vegetables) or by cutting it open and checking the color and temperature (for meat).

Late for Lecture: Quick and Easy Breakfasts

Good morning, sunshine! Another day of compelling lectures, well-thought-out homework assignments, and plenty of time for leisure activities, right? (Unfortunately, books don't convey sarcasm at the expected college-student level.)

All right — it's 9:05 a.m. and you have a lecture at nine. You have two choices. One, make a run for it, be ten minutes late, and starve until lunchtime. Or two, make one of the recipes below, then run, be twelve minutes late, and shoot to the top of your class with the increased powers of concentration and analysis that a full stomach provides.

Nutritionists and moms everywhere say that breakfast is the most important meal of the day and that skipping it throws off your entire eating rhythm. Using the following recipes, you can prepare a decently nutritious, great-tasting breakfast in about five minutes, and eat it on the run to your first class.

Uh, it's already 9:07 — you'd better get going.

Breakfast Shake

The bad news is that if you don't have a blender, you're in trouble. The good news is that if you do, you can have a great-tasting breakfast every morning that fulfills all your nutritional requirements and takes about a minute to make. Best of all, shakes can be changed around indefinitely; if you don't like bananas, use strawberries, mangos, or whatever other fruit you want. Heck, use a cucumber for all we care.

The basic rules for a shake are pretty simple: about one cup of liquid to one cup of solid for a thick but drinkable shake consistency — and use nothing too hard that's going to break your blender or that you don't want to drink, like apple cores or orange rinds.

Try one of our favorite breakfast shake combinations, the Blended Peanut Butter and Banana Sandwich (see next page), and then experiment and discover your own.

Blended Peanut Butter and Banana Sandwich

Take:

½ cup milk
½ cup plain yogurt
1 tablespoon chocolate syrup or chocolate powder
1 peeled, frozen banana
3 tablespoons peanut butter

Throw it all in your blender and blend for 1-2 minutes, or until smooth.

Adding honey to a shake gives it a sweeter taste, and yogurt will give it a creamy consistency, so monkey with the addition of these ingredients according to your taste.

Besides every kind of fruit, you might want to throw in any of the following items: cinnamon, brown sugar, maple syrup, flavored yogurt, or ice cream. Also, you can try substituting soy milk of any flavor into the recipe. Soy is better for those who are lactose intolerant, comes in a variety of flavors, and as an added bonus, it doesn't spoil as quickly as regular milk.

○○○○○○○○○○○○○○○○○○○○○○○○○○○○○○

Breakfast Pita

Hundreds of years ago, while Europe was struggling through the dark ages, the Mediterranean world was striving toward a larger goal: inventing a kind of bread that's also a bag. Finally, in 1976 they succeeded, creating the pita — and the culinary world hasn't been the same since.

Nowadays, you can buy pita in any grocery store in America. You *should* buy pita for a few reasons: it's more compact than most bread, saving valuable counter/fridge space; it freezes more easily, and takes longer to spoil that way; and it can double as both meal ingredient and portable serving tray. If you ever have to run across campus with your breakfast in your hand, you'll quickly see why a breakfast pita is infinitely preferable to, say, breakfast sushi. You can lug a pita with one hand, and when it's done, there's no garbage left over.

You can, of course, fill your breakfast pita with just about anything. Here is one suggestion: Huevos Rancheros in Your Hand.

Huevos Rancheros in Your Hand

One of the greatest secrets of the experienced cook: you can scramble an egg in less time than it takes to pour and eat a bowl of cereal. Add some melted cheese, a vegetable or two, maybe even a bit of meat, throw it all in a pita, and you've got yourself a substantial breakfast.

Ingredients:

cooking spray
2 eggs
herbs
a dash of milk
3 tablespoons cheese
3 tablespoons salsa
pita

1. Put your frying pan on the stove and turn up the burner until it's on about as high as it'll go. Spray the pan with cooking spray or use a tablespoon of vegetable oil or butter.

2. While the pan heats up, crack the eggs into a small bowl or drinking cup. Take a fork and stir them around until the yolk and the white combine. Throw in oregano, pepper, or any other herbs to spice up the taste of the eggs.

3. (Optional) Add a touch of milk to fluff up the eggs and make them a little prettier.

4. Cut a slit along the top of your pita, creating a pocket.

5. When the pan's sizzling, turn the heat down to a medium heat and throw on the eggs. Stir them around for a bit. When they start to solidify, throw the cheese and salsa on top. Stir again.

6. In about 2 or 3 minutes, the eggs should fully solidify and start to turn a little brown around the edges. That means you're done. Turn off the heat, dump the mixture in the pita and throw the pan under water in the sink. Now grab your books with one hand and the pita with the other, and sprint for class.

More Information on Making Eggs

...is in "The Fundamentals" chapter on page 44. Take a look!

On-the-Go Apple Salad

Fruit is a classic no-time-for-breakfast breakfast, but fruit alone can't really satisfy your early morning need for energy. Thankfully, though, Mother Nature crafted the apple as a sturdy breakfast carrying-case that can be filled with all sorts of hunger-beating ingredients. Try the recipe below and then use whatever else you like to charge it up.

1 large apple
plain or flavored yogurt
breakfast cereal/granola
cinnamon

1. Core the apple. To do this, set it down on a cutting board right side up, and plunge a knife through it from top to bottom, somewhere near the center. Then cut around in a circle until the center slides out. For the purpose of this recipe, cutting a wider hole in the center is better, and that makes it easier and quicker to do.

2. Slice off about half an inch from the bottom end of the center piece that just slid out. This will be used to cap the bottom of the hollowed-out apple.

3. Place cap in the bottom of the apple and then fill the hollow center first with a bit of yogurt, then some cereal and cinnamon, and top it off with some more yogurt.

It's as easy as that. Other ingredients you might want to throw into your portable salad include chopped up pieces of other fruits — oranges, bananas, whatever — as well as peanut butter, chocolate chips, honey, chocolate or maple syrup, and cream cheese or bits of solid cheese. Try, for instance, peanut butter with cereal and a bit of chocolate syrup or cream cheese, banana, and honey.

Already Done Pancakes

Believe it or not, pancakes can be made quickly enough to fit into even the tightest early-morning schedule. If you can take just five minutes at night to mix up your batter and leave it in the fridge, you can have pancakes the next morning in just a few minutes.

Ingredients:

¾ cup flour
1 tablespoon sugar
½ teaspoon salt
1 teaspoon baking powder
1 egg
¾ cup milk

1. Mix all the dry ingredients together in a bowl.
2. Slowly add egg and milk to the dry mixture, stirring it around until you get a thick liquid batter.
3. Cover the batter with plastic wrap and leave it in the fridge.

In the morning:

1. Put a pan on high heat and spray it with cooking spray.
2. While it's heating, take out the batter and toss in some chocolate chips, pecans, apple slices, or banana chunks.
3. Make small, silver-dollar style pancakes and they'll cook faster. When the edges of the cake turn brown, flip it over and cook the other side.
4. When you're done, throw the pan into the sink and douse the pancakes in butter or syrup, as you like.

It's possible — though difficult, quite dangerous, and pretty stupid — to perform an amazing task of time-efficiency while cooking your pancakes. Start a large pancake going on a medium-low heat before you hop in the shower, take a short, five-minute shower, and reappear in your kitchen just in time to flip it over. Then, quickly throw on your clothes and again make it back just in time to take the pancake off before it burns. If you're crazy enough to try this, please do time everything out (both your showering/dressing time and the pancake's cooking time) on several trial runs in advance, maybe on a Sunday morning. Your roommates will think you're crazy, of course, but if it means the difference between a hot nutritious breakfast and no breakfast at all, it's worth a shot.

Already Half-Done Hash Browns

There's nothing like some golden fried hash browns to get you going in the morning. Like the Already Done Pancakes, the key here is to put in a little work the night before. In this case, you can do the job while you watch TV or even — heaven forbid! — do some of that reading that's been piling up on your desk since September.

1. Boil a pot of water, large enough to fit as many potatoes as you're going to want — two medium-sized potatoes should be more than enough to feed you.

2. Once the water is good and boiling, drop the potatoes in and let them sit for about 15 minutes.

3. Take the pot off the stove, empty the hot water into the sink, and fill it back up with cold water. This "shocks" the potatoes — in other words, it makes them stop cooking.

4. Put them in the freezer for 10 minutes to cool them off.

5. Slice up the potatoes into appropriately-sized chunks and put them into a bowl. Cover in plastic wrap or in a plastic bag, and leave them in the fridge.

In the morning:

1. Heat up a pan on the highest heat. Throw in some cooking oil, enough to lightly cover the surface of the pan.

2. While the pan heats, mix some herbs and spices and maybe some chopped onion or garlic in with your potato chunks.

3. Put the hash brown mixture on the pan and stir it around while it fries. It should take about 5 minutes until all the pieces turn golden brown.

And that's it. Hash browns with a bit of meat or cheese and some ketchup or barbecue sauce added to them also make another great filling for a breakfast pita.

A Good Recipe for French Toast

...is not in this chapter, but on page 88 instead. You should check it out.

"Not a Chickwich *Again*": Defeating Institutional Lunch

It's amazing, the appetite you can build up while sleeping through lectures and doodling in your notebooks instead of taking notes. College is *hard work*. And hard work like that demands an energizing meal at midday that won't bloat you, but will refresh you enough for another round of ignoring your professors.

The problem is that college cafeterias and snack bars often take their instructions from the OPEC oil cartel: keep demand high, supply low, and prices cruel. Sometimes that last box of refrigerated sushi from 1982 isn't exactly your idea of a fulfilling lunch, and at $9.50, it's not winning any prizes for value. Your seventh cafeteria chickwich in as many days may force you to seriously consider food-deprivation as a viable option.

If you can't get back to your apartment during the school day, you can always pack a convenient, tasty lunch that won't let you down like that squat, hairy woman in the Social Sciences building who doles out the mystery meat. In this chapter are guidelines for packable, satisfying lunches that you can prepare the morning before class — or more likely, the night before.

OOOOOOOOOOOOOOOOOOOOOOOOOOOOOOOOOO

Basic Sandwiches

Let's all take a moment to consider the Earl of Sandwich. Here's a guy — British probably, with a title like that — who gets his name remembered for the rest of history for probably the most inane "discovery" imaginable. "Hey, look — if I take two pieces of bread and put some stuff in the middle, I can eat the stuff without getting my hands all dirty!" Well, bully for you, Earl. You're right up there with Einstein and Edison, aren't you?

The truth is, though, that despite its dubious worth as a scientific discovery, the sandwich does taste pretty good. And it's easy enough for even the most kitchen-phobic chef to experiment with. Out of pure respect for you, dear reader, we're going to assume that you've got the basics of sandwich preparation down pat: take two pieces of bread, stick some filling in the middle, and eat. But we will help you with some of the inside secrets of experienced sandwich-makers everywhere.

First, and simplest, bread. Any bread will do for sandwich bread, as long as you can slice it into an acceptable thickness and length. French baguettes work wonders, Italian foccaccia bread is all the rage at small sandwich shops, and you can roll up cold or hot ingredients into a tortilla to form a wrap, but plain old white bread still holds its own. You may want to cut off crusts or toast the bread in advance. If you'll be eating in a busy place where you might not get to sit down, you may want to consider a one-piece bread that folds over into sandwich form. Long rolls like baguettes can be slit up the side and stuffed, and pita, the Mediterranean wonder bread, works perfectly as a stuffed-sandwich bread. This will make your lunch less sloppy, as the filling can only fall out in one direction — into your mouth.

Speaking of filling — this is where things get complex. Traditional favorites include pastrami, roast beef, veggies and cheese, tuna salad, egg salad, chicken salad, chicken breast, turkey, smoked salmon and cream cheese, cold cuts like salami and bologna, et cetera, et cetera. Recently, sandwich shops have pushed the bread envelope, throwing every kind of fruit and vegetable in with every kind of cold meat and every kind of sauce.

In this section, we'll outline a few of the most basic sandwich preparations we can think of — how to make a good tuna salad and egg salad — and we'll give you a couple of our favorite combinations, but we'll leave the experimentation up to you. Making the perfect sandwich for you is all about using your favorite ingredients. Check out "The Fundamentals," starting on page 48, for sauces and salad dressings you can throw into your sandwiches. Try, for instance, making a sandwich with pesto or Caesar dressing and use any veggies you like with any meats or cheeses to create your favorite type of sandwich. Remember that anything a high-priced sandwich shop can make, you can make cheaper and better by buying in quantity at the supermarket.

Tuna Salad

Take:

1 can tuna in water
salt and pepper/herbs and spices
optional: 1 tablespoon mayonnaise
optional: 1 stalk celery or 1 carrot, finely chopped
optional: lemon juice
any other vegetables you want to throw in

Basically, open the can, drain out the water, stir up the tuna with mayonnaise and any other ingredients you'd like in your tuna salad, and you're done.

A note on tuna in oil versus tuna in water: One is fairly nutritious, the other is a nutritional nightmare. Tuna in oil has almost twice the calories as its water-packed cousin, ten times the fat, and six times the saturated fat. Having a can of oil-packed tuna once in a while certainly isn't going to kill you, but the nutritional difference is significant enough that, unless you have a fat-deficiency in your diet, you should opt for the water-packed.

Egg Salad

Some people like egg-salad sandwiches, while some people think chopped egg smells a little like a festering pool of sulfur. If you're in the latter camp, you may want to avoid following the instructions below:

1. Hard-boil an egg. That means you need to boil a pot of water, then throw the egg in and let it *boil* until the inside of the egg turns *hard*. (Isn't it amazing, this innovative cooking vocabulary?) It should take about 10 minutes. (See "The Fundamentals" on page 45 if you'd like to see these instructions rephrased longwindedly.)

2. Once that's done, take the shell off the hard-boiled egg and then separate the egg white (the white part) from the yolk (the yellow part). You can separate them easily by cutting down the center of the egg and then popping the yolk out from inside the white.

3. Mash the yolk up with about a teaspoon's worth of mayonnaise or plain yogurt and then add the egg white and mash it all together. If you like, chop some vegetables into little pieces and mix that in with the egg salad.

4. Add the chopped egg to bread with whatever toppings you like — we recommend lettuce and a slice of tomato — and you've got yourself a professional quality egg-salad sandwich.

Examples of Our Favorite Creative Sandwiches

Here are some sandwiches that we happen to like. You don't have to like them; you don't even have to try them. But we hope they'll give you a few ideas of how you can combine ingredients to make your sandwiches something you look forward to. We're not going to tell you how to make them, either. We're just going to give you the ingredients and assume that you can negotiate the process of getting them onto bread.

Pizza Sandwich

baguette, sliced and folded open
homemade mild tomato salsa
fresh mozzarella cheese
grated parmesan cheese
grilled mushrooms and onions
fried salami

Greek Sandwich

toasted foccacia bread
lettuce
black and green olives
crumbled feta cheese
bean sprouts

Now, stop relying on us and start being creative. Go make a sandwich right now with stuff you've got in your kitchen.

Portable, Microwavable Lunch

Many student centers, cafeterias, and even libraries on campuses seem to be stocking microwaves these days. And while the phrase "The world is your kitchen!" should not be taken fully literally (i.e., please do not start walking around the world in your boxer shorts, drinking maple syrup straight from the bottle), you might as well take advantage of the facilities provided for you. So here's a quick idea for a portable lunch that's not just another sandwich.

You'll need:

a good sized potato
some plastic wrap
other stuff: cheese, mushrooms, bacon bits, or whatever

1. At home, poke a lot of deep holes into your potato with a fork. This makes it easier for the heat to get in, or get out, or something.
2. Bake it in your microwave for 5 minutes on high or in your oven at 450° Fahrenheit for 30 minutes.
3. Take out the potato and let it cool off a bit.
4. When it's cooled down, cut the potato lengthwise down the center — not completely, so that the two halves are still connected — and then fill the opening with cheese, mushrooms, bacon bits, or whatever. (If you're going to use broccoli, you've got to boil it first until it's soft.)
5. Wrap up the potato in plastic wrap so that it won't leak in your knapsack.
6. Throw the potato, in the plastic wrap, into the microwave at the cafeteria or library for a minute or two until the cheese melts and the potato is hot.
7. Peel off the hot plastic, and eat.

And there you have it — finally a use for those public microwaves. Of course, using the same principle, you can heat up your sandwiches or wraps.

The Fundamentals: How to Make Dinner 76 Nights in a Row

Meat, Vegetables, and Pasta are about as fundamental to college cooking as Truth, Liberty, and Justice are to France. But like the streets of Paris, when standards aren't maintained and watched over with patience and vigilance, they can start to stink.

If you aren't bored yet of the basic college recipes inevitably prepared at one time or another by every student in America, then you soon will be. This chapter will show you how to spice up and change the standards with almost no effort at all using the ingredients you probably already have.

This chapter is split into two parts. The first outlines the methods of preparing some of the basic, standard dinner-type foods. The second gives recipes for many tasty, easy-to-prepare sauces that can be added to any of the basic meals.

Preparation Techniques

When you really come down to it, you can know the flavors and tastes of every herb and spice in the book; you can know how to combine different ingredients to create a symphony of flavors in your mouth; you can be an expert at presenting your creations beautifully, making each plate a small work of art; but still — if you undercook the chicken, you'll be sick all night.

Flavor is important, don't get us wrong. But if you have no substance to combine that flavor with, then you've got no meal. That's why you have to become comfortable with chicken breasts, a samurai of stir-fry, and the high priest of potatoes. You have to become one with your ingredients so that you can prepare meals without blinking.

We'll go through ingredients and techniques one by one so that next time you're making dinner, if you start to feel nervous, you can just flip open to this section and it'll guide you through whatever you've started doing so that you don't mess it up too badly. And now, with no fear, grab the nearest hunk of food and start cooking!

Filets and Steaks

What we're talking about here are slabs of meat. They can be thicker or thinner, they can come from any number of animals, they can have big hunks of bone in them or no bones at all. But they're just hunks of meat, and you're going to want to cook them.

If you're lazy — and as a college student, you should be — you'll probably want to buy mostly filets, because then you've paid someone to take out the bones, which you really, really don't want to eat. Either way, though, here's how to do your basic pregame preparation:

1. If you've decided to freeze your meat — which is a good call unless you plan to eat it on the same day you bring it home from the supermarket — you'll need to thaw it out. You can do this by leaving it in the fridge for several hours (you should take out meat for dinner in the morning) or by using your microwave's defrost function (it should have instructions for different sizes and kinds of meat). You can also put the meat in a sealed plastic bag and run warm (not very hot) water over it in the sink.
2. Separate each filet and wash it by running it under the tap.
3. Cut off any undesirable parts of the filet. If you see big, gross, hardened white spots in the meat (fat) or red blood spots, you can just cut them out. Don't cut away too much; most of the undesirable parts will cook away. But basically, cut out any part you don't want to eat.

Now, you'll want to cook the meat in any one of the following ways:

Marinated

Take a look at the "Basic Marinades" section of the "Sauces" part of this chapter (page 50) for some ideas on what kind of marinades to make. Basically, though, you want to follow these steps:

1. Prepare a marinade.
2. Place the filets/steaks in the marinade so that they're covered on all sides. They don't need to be drowning in the stuff, but at least well-coated.
3. Seal them in a container with a lid or cover the bowl with plastic wrap. Leave to marinate for at least 1 hour if left open on the countertop, or overnight (about ten hours) in the fridge.
4. When the meat is thoroughly marinated, remove the filets/steaks and let the excess marinade drip off them. The flavor should be absorbed into the meat by now, so you don't need the sauce on the outside.

5. Cook the meat. Preheat a pan or the oven. No need to add oil, because the marinade should be enough to lubricate the pan and keep the meat from burning. If frying in a pan over medium-high heat, times are approximately:
   - Beef filet (a piece about 2-3 cm or ¾-1¼ inches thick): on each side, 3-4 minutes for rare, 4-5 for medium, 5-7 for well-done
   - Beef steak (sirloin or rump, about 2 cm or ¾ inch thick): about a half-minute less on each side than the time for a beef filet
   - Pork: sliced tenderloin filets (about 1 cm or ½ inch thick): 2-4 minutes on each side
   - Lamb chops (2 cm or ¾ inch thick): 2-4 minutes on each side
   - Chicken breasts (2 cm or ¾ inch thick): 3-5 minutes on each side
   - Fish filets: 2-3 minutes on each side per centimeter or half-inch of thickness, until the fish flakes easily with a fork

Leftover meat that has been marinated and cooked can be wrapped up and kept in the fridge for a couple of days. You can warm it up and eat it straight, use it as a sandwich filling hot or cold, or throw it on top of a salad. In other words, make more than you need, and you can use it later.

Breaded

(This is the same procedure as for "Fried, Battered Anything" on page 79 of the "'Anybody Got a Hairnet?'" chapter. You know why? Because meat counts as "anything.")

The Germans, and lots of other people, call breaded meat "schnitzel." You don't need to be able to pronounce *unterwachtmeister*, though, to make a good breaded chicken breast. All you need to do is:

1. Make your breading mixture by crushing up or blending either bread or crackers. Then add some salt and pepper and other spices.
2. Crack an egg (or two, if you've got a lot of meat) and stir it up with 1 tablespoon of water until it's uniform.
3. Dip your filets in the egg, then roll them around in the crumb mixture until they're nicely coated. Fry them in a pan with a couple tablespoons of oil.
4. The approximate cooking times are the same as above. But just to make things easy, here they are again:
   - Beef filet (a piece about 2-3 cm or ¾-1¼ inches thick): on each side, 3-4 minutes for rare, 4-5 for medium, 5-7 for well-done
   - Beef steak (sirloin or rump, about 2 cm or ¾ inch thick): about a half-minute less on each side than the time for a beef filet

- Pork: sliced tenderloin filets (about 1 cm or ½ inch thick): 2-4 minutes on each side
- Lamb chops (2 cm or ¾ inch thick): 2-4 minutes on each side
- Chicken breasts (2 cm or ¾ inch thick): 3-5 minutes on each side
- Fish filets: 2-3 minutes on each side per centimeter or half-inch of thickness, or until the fish flakes easily with a fork

Stir-Fried

A vegetable stir-fry isn't bad, but it doesn't compare to a solid veggie-and-meat stir-fry. Filets make perfect stir-fry additions if you slice them up into bite-sized chunks. For veggies, see the information on stir-frying vegetables in the "Vegetables" section (page 47) to know approximately how long you'll need to stir-fry them for. Basically, here's a rough procedure for stir-frying:

1. Cut up the chicken, beef, or pork filets into little bite-sized pieces and add them to the pan. Cook these for about 5 minutes, stirring around now and again.
2. Add onions, carrots, and/or chunks of potato. Keep stirring and cooking for another 3 minutes.
3. Add peppers, corn niblets, snow peas, bean sprouts, and/or asparagus. Cook for about 2 minutes.
4. Add a splash of soy sauce, maple syrup, fresh pressed garlic, and/or fresh or dried herbs. Cook for another minute and you're done.

OOOOOOOOOOOOOOOOOOOOOOOOOOOOOOOOOO

Ground Meat

As convenient as filets are, they don't even come close to ground meat. Ground meat is simple to make, tastes like meat (because it is), and will fill you up. You can mix it with almost anything and in almost any way, and it'll still be good.

When you bring home ground meat from the market, you'll probably want to freeze it. And when you decide that you'd like to eat it, you'll probably want to unfreeze it. (Unless you're really curious what a meat-popsicle tastes like.) Defrost it the same way you'd defrost steaks — either in the microwave with the defrost function, in the fridge for several hours, or in a sealed plastic bag under warm water.

No need to wash the ground beef because it should already be decently clean and when heated up, any germs will be killed anyway. You should remember to pour off excess fat as you cook your ground beef.

So, moving right along, you've got a couple choices:

Hamburgers and Meatballs

Preparing hamburgers and meatballs is similar, but the cooking is different. The first step is to prepare the meat so that it'll stick together in ball or patty form so that you can cook it. The way to do this is to add other substances to the meat that'll make it sticky. Also, now is the time to season the meat with any number of additions. Once you've made one of the mixes below, shape the meat into balls or patties as you like, then cook with the cooking times shown below.

1 pound ground meat
½ packet onion soup mix
1-2 tablespoons sour cream
herbs and spices

OR

1 pound ground meat
1 egg, stirred around and then added to the meat
½ cup breadcrumbs
salt, pepper, herbs and spices

Cooking times:

- Burgers should be 1-2 cm (½-¾ inches) thick, and should be cooked for 4-6 minutes on each side. Check that your burgers are done by cutting into them and seeing if the color is the same throughout the burger.
- Meatballs: 90 minutes in a pot with sauce, on low heat (bring the sauce to a boil first and then lower the heat) — or 15 minutes on a baking tray in the oven at 300° Fahrenheit.

Tacos, Chili, Fajitas, etc.

If you don't feel like molding your ground meat into balls or patties, your other option is to leave it loose. All you've got to do then is cook it with whatever else you want to eat it with. Again, you can stir-fry ground meat with vegetables. Just use the following cooking times to know when to add the meat (and look at page 47 for the vegetable cooking instructions). You can also fry the meat alone and put it in taco shells or tortillas along with toppings. Or you can mix the fried meat with beans, tomatoes, and other veggies in a thick sauce and make yourself a chili. (See page 87 for the recipe for bean chili, and then add meat.) Basically, here are the approximate cooking times for different ground meats; what you do with them once they're cooked is truly up to you.

Cooking time for about 225 grams (8 ounces) of meat:

- Ground beef/chicken/veal/pork: 2-4 minutes for the meat, plus 2 more minutes with whatever else you're adding

A couple notes: Just to remind you again — see how concerned we are for your health? — it's not necessary to add oil to a pan before frying up ground meat because usually the meat has enough oil and fat of its own. In fact, it'll probably have so much that after you've fried it for a while you should drain off the excess fat into a jar. Second, go ahead and throw in whatever flavors or other ingredients you like with the meat. If you like it spicy, add chili powder. If you like it sweet, maple syrup does wonders.

Rice and Pasta

Oh, carbohydrates! What would the inexperienced and cheap chef ever do without them? With rice and pasta, you can fill yourself up without a lot of work, and though they're kind of plain, you can add absolutely anything to them to make them taste better. Plus, they're cheap and it's next to impossible to screw them up.

Pasta

The basic technique for making pasta is:

1. Boil enough water so the pasta will have plenty of space to float around. Add just a bit of salt (about a teaspoon for every 2 liters/3.5 pints). If you add a couple drops of vegetable or olive oil, the pasta won't stick and the water won't boil over.
2. Add pasta to the boiling water, stirring every once in a while, but especially at the beginning so that it doesn't stick to the bottom of the pot.
3. Wait until it is as soft as you want it (you can just spear a couple noodles with a fork and try them every couple minutes), which will probably take between 5 and 15 minutes.
4. Remove pasta from water (this is best done with a strainer).
5. Flavor pasta (i.e., add sauce) and eat.

Different kinds of pasta take different lengths of time: spaghetti takes about 8 or 9 minutes, vermicelli about 5 minutes, and spirals or rotini 7 or 8 minutes. Of course, these are approximate times, and there's no better way to tell than by just trying a couple noodles.

See the "Sauces" section of this chapter on page 48 for ideas on what to do with your pasta.

Casseroles

Casseroles were discovered when someone once put their pasta dish in the oven by mistake. They're sort of like pasta pies, and they're good. They'll also save for a couple days, so they make sense for you to make. Once you've boiled your pasta, you can make a casserole really easily. Just do this:

1. Mix your cooked pasta with any one or more of the following casserole fillings in a deep bowl or cake pan or casserole dish: tuna fish from a can, fried ground meat, or just tomato sauce and cheese. (If you just add cheese, you're technically not making a casserole but something closer to a lasagna or baked ziti dish — but who cares about technicalities, right?) Layer the top with cheese.
2. Bake the thing in the oven on a high heat, about 450° Fahrenheit, until it's nice and crunchy on top and mushy in the middle. This should take about 30 minutes, depending on how big it is, but keep checking every 5 minutes to make sure you don't dry it out too much.

When it's done, bring it out of the oven and let it cool a bit. Cut it out like you'd cut pieces of cake, making sure you allocate at least a little of the baked-cheese crust with each piece.

Rice

If you like things that are popular, you'll probably love rice. Literally billions of people around the world eat rice every day — and this is your chance to join the club!

The ratio for cooking rice is about 1 cup of rice to 2 cups of water, with about 1 teaspoon of salt per cup of rice. You don't need to use standard cups in this case, of course, so long as the ratio is correct (and you can estimate with the salt). And you should know that rice puffs up to about four times its size when you cook it, so be sure to approximate how much you'll need.

Throw the rice and water together in a pot and bring it to a boil (without a cover). Then cover the pot and reduce the heat to low and let it sit until the rice gets soft; it should take about 20 minutes for a cup of rice. After the 20 minutes, turn the heat off and let the pot sit for 5 minutes before you lift the lid.

Like pasta, you can add anything to rice to make it more interesting. It works especially well as a base for a stir-fry, filling you up while taking on the flavors of the vegetables and meat. Soy sauce and rice generally work well together, and even plain rice with tiny pieces of fried onion work great.

Potatoes

Potatoes hold a sacred place in the kitchen. If you need any evidence, look in an encyclopedia under "The Great Irish Potato Famine." Think about it: would there ever be a "Great Swedish Donut Famine?" Probably not. A "Great Brazilian Parsley Famine?" No, because potatoes are different. They are meals in themselves and perfect additions to any meal. They are easy to cook, can be done in many different ways, and are satisfying and tasty — and cheap.

If stored in a cool, dark place, potatoes can last quite a while. When you're ready to use them, take them out of storage, wash them (just run them under water and scrub any dirt and growths off the surface with your hand), and then you're ready to use any of the following cooking techniques.

A note on skins: By all means, if you don't like potato skins, take them off. But skins are healthy and we think they add a nice texture to mashed potatoes and other such dishes. So, do whatever you want — but we say leave the skins on.

Roasted

Roasting potatoes takes some time, but it's pretty easy to set them roasting and then not worry about them while you make the rest of dinner.

1. Cut the potatoes into good-sized pieces and rinse them with water.
2. Find yourself a baking dish of some kind — a very shallow pot or something similar. Coat the bottom of it in just a touch of olive oil.
3. Heat up the dish in your oven to a pretty high heat, about 425° Fahrenheit.
4. Dry the potatoes. Then, scratch up their surfaces a bit with a fork. This'll help the outsides get crunchy. Put them in the hot dish, turning them over a few times so that they get coated in oil.
5. Roast them for about 1 hour until they're golden on all sides, turning once every 15 minutes.

If you can time this right with the finish of your dinner, you'll have hot, roasted potatoes as a perfect side dish to whatever else you're making.

Baked

Nothing is simpler than making a baked potato. Do this:

1. Put the potato in the oven on a high heat, around 450° Fahrenheit. You can wrap it in tinfoil if you like. You can also poke a couple holes in the potato with a fork and nuke it on a high heat in your microwave for about 5 minutes.
2. When it's baked (probably about 30 minutes later) take it out and eat it.

Now, just telling you that much would be a pretty big waste of time. So we have a couple of tips. One is that the next time you're near a hardware store, drop in and pick up a couple of aluminum nails. Bring them home and clean them up (boil a pot of water and drop the nails in for five minutes) and then you've got a great tool for speeding up the potato-baking process. Just insert the nail into the potato before baking in the oven, and the metal will conduct heat into the center, making the baking process quicker and more even. Note that this works only in ovens and toaster ovens, and not — NOT! — in microwaves. Microwaves don't like metal objects, and putting a big metal nail in your microwave will probably lead it to have a pretty serious spasm. So don't do it.

The second tip is that plain baked potatoes taste like, well, potatoes. And that's not bad, but you probably will want to add one or more of the following: butter, salt and pepper, sour cream, steamed broccoli, melted cheese, sautéed mushrooms and onions, fried bacon bits, or whatever.

Make one and it's a substantial snack; make two and it's a large meal; make ten and it's a low-intensity dinner party.

Mashed

Mashed potatoes have been making a serious comeback and it looks like they're here to stay. Diners serve them; fancy restaurants serve them; our moms still serve them. There's no reason why you shouldn't.

Use a potato or two for every person you're going to feed.

1. Cut them into several pieces each to make them boil quicker. Boil them in enough water so that the potatoes are submerged, and add a teaspoon of salt to the water.
2. After 15-20 minutes, drain the water out.
3. Add 1 teaspoon butter and 2 teaspoons milk (or cream if you've got it) per potato. Or more, or less, depending on how creamy you like your potatoes. You can also add a few garlic cloves, some melted cheese, or other little things like that.
4. Mash. Crush. Destroy. Pound those potatoes into creamy, smooth oblivion. (If you don't have a potato masher — and you probably don't — make sure you use something sturdy, like a big wooden spoon or one of those useless ninety-dollar science textbooks.)
5. Season with salt, pepper, herbs and spices, and eat.

And, of course, mashed potatoes present an excellent opportunity for post-cooking creativity. Mold your mound of potatoes into a diorama of Mt. Rushmore for extra credit in your Political Science class — or use them to make a sculpture of the DNA molecule for your bio professor. We're sure you'll be the coolest kid in class.

Fried

If you're looking for how to make french fries, you've come to the wrong place. Trust us, it's not that we don't know how, but it's that you can get fries anywhere you go and if you were to bother making them at home it would take you way more time and effort than frying up a batch of larger-cut potatoes. You can call them home-style fries if you like; you can call them whatever you like as far as we're concerned, so long as you make them and like them.

Frying potatoes works the same as frying anything else. Get a pan going on high heat (about 450°) with some oil, then throw the potato pieces in and fry them up. This tends to take a while, though, so you might want to boil the potatoes in water for 15 minutes before you start frying them. They're done when they turn golden brown, and you can add whatever you want. Even ketchup. Even though they're not french fries.

▽△

Eggs

Some may argue that eggs don't really belong in a chapter about dinner, but we don't care — they taste great, are very filling, and are simple to make. If you want, eat them for dinner. If not, just turn down the corner of this page and flip to it when you're making breakfast.

The only problem with eggs is thinking about what they are, biologically speaking. If you can get around that, eggs are the perfect food for the college chef: cheap, easy to make, and incredibly diverse. You can start with two identical eggs and end up with two dishes that aren't similar at all.

Note: There are about a hundred thousand puns and lame jokes to make about eggs. Despite the fact that this book tries to be funny, we're not going to sink to the level of any of those clichés. We're just going to tell you how to make good eggs.

Also note: Health experts warn that eggs, when eaten raw, can be dangerous. So you generally shouldn't eat raw eggs or things with raw eggs in them. But you might like your fried eggs runny. Are you going to get sick from that, you ask? Good question. The answer is probably not. Most of the eggs you buy in the store are not going to have salmonella bacteria and give you food poisoning. Of course, a tiny percentage of the eggs you buy may be dangerous, but unless you make a habit of eating or drinking raw eggs — and you shouldn't — then you'll most likely be fine. And the truth is, a little food poisoning would be a horrible, horrible experience, but you might survive. No guarantees from us, though — in general, you take your life in your own hands when you follow the directions this book is giving you, anyway.

Hard-Boiled

These are great because they're not messy, you can take them with you for lunch or a snack, and you can easily separate out the yolk and not eat it if you feel like being health-conscious. To boil an egg effectively, here are some important tips:

- Boil the water first, add some salt, and then add the eggs.
- Be careful dropping the eggs into the water; if you drop them too fast they'll hit the bottom and break.
- Eggs should be room temperature when you add them to the water; otherwise, they run a higher risk of cracking.
- Boil for about 8-10 minutes for hard-boiled. If you prefer soft-boiled eggs, leave them in for about 5 minutes.
- Cool off the eggs in cold water from the tap when you're done boiling them so that you won't burn your fingers while you peel.
- Peel before eating. If you roll the egg along a countertop before peeling, the shell will come off more easily.

If you don't like plain boiled eggs, you can always mash up hard-boiled eggs into a quick egg salad (see page 33) or you can remove the yolks, mash that up into a salad with some cut up vegetables, and then reinsert the mixture into the egg whites.

Fried Eggs

Eggs fried with their yolk facing up are called "Sunny Side Up." If you flip the egg over once it's been cooking, it's called "Over Easy." You can make either of these kinds of eggs. Just grease up a pan with a bit of oil (maybe 1 teaspoon's worth) and heat it up. Then crack the egg into the pan (break it by hitting it against the side of the pan, and then use your thumbs on each side of the crack to split it open) and let it sit there. Some people prefer their yolks runny and some prefer their yolks hard. Fry the egg until it's as hard as you like it. If you use a low to medium heat, it'll take longer, but it'll cook through without the bottom getting too brown.

Scrambled Eggs and Omelets

In their most basic form, scrambled eggs are just fried eggs that have been shaken up a lot. To make them, use a fork to stir up a couple eggs in a small bowl with:

1 tablespoon milk per egg
salt and pepper to taste

Again, cook these on a low heat with a little oil. One good trick is to use a spatula to drag the eggs from the edges of the pan into the center. This helps the eggs cook evenly and still leaves the proper, unstirred texture. They're done when they're not runny anymore.

For omelets, make the same egg, milk, and salt and pepper mixture and cook it similarly — just don't drag the egg into the center. Rather, lift the mixture a little so that the uncooked eggs will spread out and get time touching the pan. Let the eggs lie flat and solidify a bit, and then put bits of cheese, chopped vegetables, meat, etc, on top of one half of the eggs. When the eggs have solidified even more, flip the uncovered side of the omelet on top of the covered side to seal the ingredients in. Then cook the omelet a little longer, flipping it over to give equal time to both top and bottom.

Vegetables

There are a lot of different kinds of vegetables. Really a *lot*. Many of them are good. Some of them are gross. We're not going to tell you which are which, though — you'll have to figure that out for yourself.

In this section, we'll try to tell you the ground rules for cooking different kinds of vegetables. Then you're on your own. You can mix it up and use a bunch of different vegetables in each meal, or you can just eat a lot of one thing. We don't care.

Also, don't stress when you're cooking vegetables. Don't stress in general, but with vegetables, as long as you wash them and cut off the gross looking parts, they're probably not going to make you sick no matter what you do with them. So, if you like your cooked carrots really hard, then don't cook them a lot, and that's fine.

Steamed

To steam vegetables, you're going to need a strainer. All you've got to do is balance that strainer on top of a pot of boiling water so that the bottom of the strainer is above the surface of the water. In other words, none of the vegetables that you put on the strainer are going to be in the water. Wash and then cut your vegetables into manageable bite-sized pieces, and then load them in the strainer and cover the top of the whole thing with a pot lid.

Approximate steaming times for a few vegetables:
Green beans: 5-10 minutes
Broccoli: 10 minutes
Carrots: 10 minutes
Cauliflower: 10 minutes
Pumpkin: 20 minutes
Sweet Potato: 10 minutes

Boiled
Boiling should be self-explanatory already. If it's not: first, boil a big pot of water. Then put stuff in it for a while. Understood? Great.

Once again — and despite the fact that they're being put into nature's cleanser, boiling water — you should remove any big gross chunks before boiling. This includes cornhusks.

Approximate boiling times for some other vegetables:
Asparagus: 5-10 minutes
Corn: 10 minutes
Potatoes: 15 minutes

Stir-Fried (which is the same, pretty much, as just plain fried)
For stir-fries, get a big pan — or ideally, a wok. Get a couple teaspoons of oil going in it on a high heat and then add the vegetables that take longest to cook: onions, potatoes, or carrots. *Stir* them around while they *fry* (hence the name!) so that some parts don't get more cooked than others. Somehow, the movement of the pieces of food gives them flavor, so keep them moving around.

When the long-cooking vegetables have begun to soften up (between 5 and 10 minutes), add other vegetables that take less time to cook — peppers, snow peas, green beans, etc., and some soy sauce or other sauces (see the "Sauces" part of this chapter for some ideas). Fry these for another couple minutes and add garlic and ginger 1-2 minutes before the end.

Of course, small strips or bite-sized pieces of chicken, pork, beef or any other meat go great in stir-fries. Depending on how well-done you like your meat to be, you should add it at approximately the same time as peppers and other middle-length-cooking vegetables.

Roasted or Grilled
There is a difference between these two: we just don't know or care what it is. Roasting/grilling works well for peppers, tomatoes, garlic, beets, and other things that are fundamentally mushy inside.

In any case, what you want to do first is preheat your oven to a medium temperature, around 300° Fahrenheit, or if you want, don't preheat your oven. Instead, once you've prepared the vegetables as outlined below, you can wrap them in tinfoil and put them on top of a barbecue grill or on your stovetop.

Wash the outside of the vegetable, then brush it with a little olive oil and sprinkle it with salt and pepper, and maybe some dried herbs and spices. Then throw it into the oven for about 10 minutes, until it's very hot and soft. Take it out of the oven, let it cool down a bit, and peel off any of the inedible parts — seeds, stems, skins, etc. Then chop it up and use it in a salad or just eat it straight up.

Sauces

There are two differences between a good chicken dinner and a bad chicken dinner. The first is the quality of the piece of chicken you use, and the second is the quality of the sauce or marinade you put on the chicken. Unfortunately, unless you're a butcher or on a very luxurious budget, you can't do much about the former. You're basically going to get as good a piece of meat as you can afford. You can, however, drastically improve the quality of your meals by preparing sauces that will make you excited for another piece, not desperate to order a pizza.

Of course, a lot of the sauces that are prepared in five-star restaurants are beyond your means — you certainly *could* make a truffle oil sauce with lobster purée, but if you do, you're going to have to pay up the nose for it. On the other hand, you can make all the sauces below with simple ingredients you have in your kitchen by simply combining them in the right proportions.

Now, this book will suggest the kinds of food you should use each sauce with. For instance, you might want to use the Caesar Dressing for a salad, or you might want to use the Classic Tomato Sauce with spaghetti. But you don't have to. You can heap Pesto on a salad or Sweet and Sour on some pasta. Experiment, mix it up, try new combinations.

Bubbie's Sweet and Sour

This unbelievable recipe could not have come from anywhere but a grandmother. "You won't believe how tasty it is until you try it," as she'd say. "Eat — eat something — you're nothing but skin and bones," she'd also say, before presenting you with a huge tray of meatballs slathered in this tangy, tasty sauce. If nothing else, the simplicity of the recipe should teach you that a little creative experimentation and improvisation can lead to a delicious surprise.

1 cup ketchup
2 cups ginger ale
garlic powder and spices to taste

1. Heat a pot on the stove to a medium heat.

2. Combine ketchup, ginger ale, and any desired garlic or spices in the pot, and stir. Let it warm for 30 minutes, stirring once every 5.

Try it with: This sauce was originally designed for beef or chicken meatballs, which can be added right into the pot and cooked in the sauce. It also goes great with chicken breasts or with ground beef in a taco.

Spicy Peanut Sauce

So much for going out for Asian food. Not that we have a problem with Szechuan flavors, but when you realize how easy it is to prepare your own Spicy Peanut Sauce from the simple ingredients you have in your kitchen, you'll probably rather stay at home and make your own dinner.

1 part peanut butter
1 part soy sauce
2 parts water
chili powder
garlic
peanuts

Mix and stir the peanut butter, soy sauce, chili powder, garlic, and peanuts in a bowl, adding more water bit by bit until you get it as thin as you want it.

Try it with: A chicken and vegetable stir-fry, or as a marinade and topping for chicken cooked on skewers with onion, peppers, and pineapple chunks. Or, for an exotic mix, throw it into a green salad with slices of orange.

The Non-Sauce

Lucky for you, one of the simplest sauces to prepare is also one of the tastiest — that's maybe why professional chefs call it The Non-Sauce. It's the kind of thing that could put them out of business. Also, they may have problems pronouncing Aglio e Olio, the traditional Italian name for this sauce. Next time you want an easy pasta sauce that's not tomato-sauce-from-a-can, try:

garlic
olive oil (use about 1½ tablespoons oil for every garlic clove)
anything else you've got: chopped tomatoes, olives, herbs, grilled vegetables, capers, etc.

1. Press or chop the garlic, then cook it in the oil for 1-2 minutes on a low heat before tossing it into the pasta.

2. Add any other ingredients you'd like to eat with your pasta.

Try it with: This is a classic pasta topping, but you can also give it a try on top of a grilled chicken breast.

Basic Marinades

Ah, if only you could study for class with the same results with which you can marinate your food. Imagine: you open all your current semester textbooks to the relevant chapters, scatter them throughout the room, and sit there on the couch soaking up the knowledge. While this would result in: a) people thinking you're weird, and b) a flamboyantly failing grade on your midterm, the cooking equivalent results in great-tasting meals.

The concept is simple — douse your food in a bath of flavor, and given enough time, it'll soak up the flavor and remain tasty when cooked. Preparing a marinade takes very little time, maybe a couple minutes. And then all you have to do is let it sit for a couple hours as the flavor seeps in. Remember that if you marinate in a container in the open air, an hour or two is sufficient. You should also try to marinate overnight in the fridge. So, if you're feeling ambitious, you can prepare tomorrow's dinner tonight and let it soak up flavor until you're ready for it. Or you can just throw something on the countertop to marinate for that night when you get home from class.

The other secret to making successful marinades is that you can use anything you want. Fruit, vegetables, and any kind of flavoring or spice are completely fair game. The stronger the flavor, the more it'll get absorbed by the marinating meat. So start with:

olive oil
salt and pepper
garlic (though you may want to leave this out now and again, both for the sake of your breath and also to give the marinade a lighter, fresher taste)
herbs

Then add any of the following (and anything else you can think of, for that matter):

chili peppers and/or powder (for a spicy marinade)
soy sauce (for Asian flavor)
mustard and Worcestershire sauce (for a proper British taste)
lime juice and pineapple (straight out of the Caribbean)
honey
orange slices
any citrus juice (see the citrus marinade on page 74 — it's simple and great)
vinegar

When you're making marinade, make enough so that it'll cover all the meat you're planning on cooking. It doesn't have to be a bath, but it needs to cover all the surfaces. Tupperware containers and shallow bowls are good vessels in which to marinate. It's also good to note that any marinade with salt, citrus fruit or juice, or vinegar will partially "cook" the meat and discolor it just a bit. This is normal and not a problem, so don't stress over it.

Try it with: You name it. Marinated chicken is a staple, but a marinade will help your steaks, pork chops, fish filets, and basically any meat you cook.

Classic Tomato Sauce

As a college student — unless you have some very peculiar tastes — you're going to need a *lot* of tomato-based sauces. You can use them for pasta, on pizza, with chicken, for bruschetta, or as salsa. Tomato sauce is like the duct tape of cooking. Again, you can start with a basic tomato sauce and throw in any vegetables, herbs, or spices you like to make your own unique concoctions.

You should probably make a lot of tomato sauce once you start making it; if you don't eat it right now, you'll probably eat it three hours from now, or tomorrow morning, or soon enough.

Note: Because there are a lot of decent premade tomato sauces on the market, you should definitely pay attention to how much you're spending on your sauce and how much you like it. It should take you about 5 minutes to prepare (and about 1-2 hours to simmer) a tomato sauce for less than half the cost of premade sauces. If you're finding it tough to accomplish that, you may want to consider buying some cheap premade sauce to have around when you are too lazy to make your own.

The simplest tomato sauce can be made with just the following ingredients:

- fresh or canned tomatoes (½ cup of diced, fresh tomatoes makes about enough sauce for 1 dish of pasta; one standard 16-oz can of crushed tomatoes should make enough sauce for about 4 dishes of pasta)
- garlic and other herbs and spices
- onions and peppers (or any vegetables you want: mushrooms, eggplant, corn, whatever)

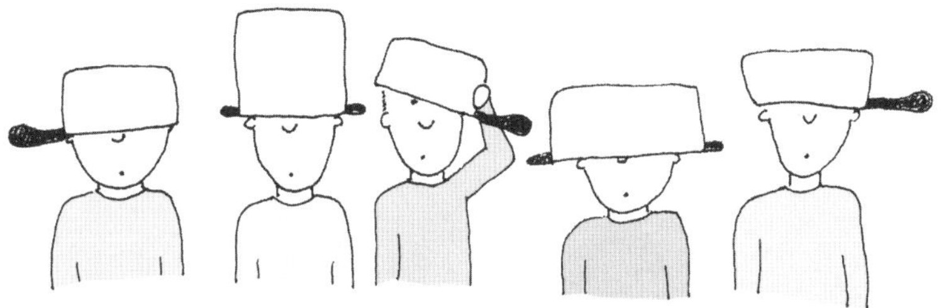

Cut up the ingredients into smaller or larger chunks according to your preference, and then simmer the sauce (let it sit over low heat) until it thickens — again, according to your taste. This can take 1-2 hours, and you'll only need to check on it and stir every 30 minutes or so.

This is, of course, only the most basic of basic tomato sauces. To give the sauce a little more of a substantial flavor, add some prebought chicken stock or broth or (cheap) white wine (about as much stock or wine as you've got tomatoes) to the sauce right at the beginning, and simmer it until the liquid has disappeared. Also, midway through your simmering, you can add grilled chicken or chunky roasted vegetables for a chunked-up sauce. Or add cream (heavy cream, table cream, or even half-and-half cream; it doesn't really matter as long as it's pretty thick) for a creamy pink rosé sauce. Or throw in some clams or mussels. Or hot peppers for a spicier sauce. Or lentils. Or — if you haven't caught on yet — anything, it doesn't really matter. As long as you have a strong base of tomatoes and basic flavors, you can add your favorite or most currently abundant ingredient to see how it will taste.

In order to use your tomato sauce for pizza, you'll probably want to blend it briefly. That'll make it easier to spread and eat. Also, if you want it to taste more like pizzeria-style pizza sauce, you should add more oregano. But by all means, experiment with a non-standard tomato sauce on a pizza: roasted eggplant sauce, blended slightly, goes great with a pizza with little roasted eggplant chunks as a topping, and grilled chicken pizza is quickly catching on.

In a sealed container in your fridge, tomato sauce will stay good (unless it has certain quick spoiling ingredients, like mussels or cream) for up to a week. So you can make some for a pasta sauce tonight, use it again tomorrow as a sauce for chicken, and then blend it up the next day as a pizza sauce.

Pesto

Pesto is one of those sauces that tastes a lot better than it looks. It looks, in fact, like nuclear-waste-infested swamp water. But if *only* nuclear-waste-infested swamp water were as useful as pesto in the kitchen! Imagine if you could use nuclear-waste-infested swamp water as a topping for pasta, for chicken, and also as a sauce for delicious, nonboring pizzas! Imagine if you served it to a friend for dinner and she said, "Wow, I've never tried nuclear-waste-infested swamp water before — but it tastes great!" Well, that's what pesto is like, except it's not horribly toxic and dangerous.

Here's how to make it. (You'll need a blender. Sorry, blender-less people. Maybe you can find a sewer full of nuclear-waste-infested swamp water or something.)

You'll need:

a whole lot of fresh basil (say, 2 decent-sized handfuls for 1 bowl of pesto)
olive oil
garlic
toasted pine nuts — to toast these, just put them in the oven on a pretty high heat and keep your eye on them until they start to turn brown

1. Blend the basil, pine nuts, and garlic. As they get blended, add the olive oil little by little, blending for a few seconds in between. Or, if you can open the top of your blender, drizzle in the oil little by little as it blends.

2. That's it.

Try it with: Like we said before — chicken, pasta, or as a stand-alone pizza sauce. Also, you could try using a different herb for a completely different taste: parsley is one idea, and you could also try something like tarragon.

Caesar Dressing

If only Julius Caesar (or whatever other Caesar it was, you smarmy history majors) knew what a legacy he would leave behind for the millennia. Not marble busts of the gods, not the Parthenon or the Acropolis — though I guess he left those, too — but one much more enduring, powerful legacy: salad dressing. Caesar salad is a worldwide favorite and a classic start to a pizza or pasta dinner. In the two thousand or so years since Caesar's death, Caesar dressings have been coming into their own, as chefs have added chicken and honey-dijon mustard to transform them from the introduction to the main event.

To make your own piece of Greco-Roman history, you'll need:

2 egg yolks
about 1 teaspoon mustard (dijon or wholegrain mustard is best)
1/4 cup wine vinegar
3/4 cup olive oil
1 garlic clove, minced

Blend or stir all the ingredients together until you get a creamy consistency. This dressing is traditionally served on romaine lettuce with croutons (just cut up bits of toasted bread), anchovies, and sprinkled generously with parmesan cheese and black pepper. Changing the lettuce won't change the taste much, and you can add bacon bits as well for a little smoky taste.

If a traditional Caesar isn't good enough for you — *Et tu, Brute?* — you can throw in some honey and an extra dose of dijon mustard for a honey-mustard Caesar that goes great with cold strips of grilled chicken. Or experiment further; try adding orange slices or some chopped walnuts, and see what your friends, Romans, and countrymen think about it.

Your Basic Non-Tomato Spicy Sauce

Let's imagine a time and place in the future in which an evil, multinational corporation has cornered the markets on tomatoes. Because of the monopoly, tomato prices have shot through the roof: say, forty thousand dollars a pound. Now, you probably still wouldn't stop eating tomato sauce — you'd just eat it less often. But anyway, here's a light, spicy sauce that you can use in case of The Great Tomato Famine.

1 part lemon juice
1 part olive oil
chili powder/cayenne pepper/Cajun spice powder/black pepper/garlic/etc.

Stir this all together until it's spicy enough for your taste. The reason this sauce works is that the lemon juice cancels out some of the oiliness of the olive oil so that it doesn't feel like you're eating a gas company's latest slip up. You can make it as spicy or mild as you want, and you can add other flavors like honey, fruits, or vegetables.

Try it with: Chicken, fish, or even burgers, as either a marinade or a sauce. Or warm it up and toss it over pasta.

Basic Vinaigrette Salad Dressing

Whether you like it or not, you're going to have to eat your vegetables. One relatively painless way to do this is with this incredibly simple salad dressing that'll make your lettuce come alive, bursting with vinaigrette flavor. Just take:

1 small garlic clove, minced
¾ cup olive or canola oil
¼ cup balsamic or wine vinegar
a little bit of dried basil
a pinch of salt and pepper

Put them all in a jar, bottle, or anything that you can seal tightly. Then just shake the dressing until it's well mixed and pour it on your salad. Beware: if you're storing it in the fridge (which you can do for up to two or three weeks), the oil and vinegar will settle quicker than a spring-semester senior with a low grade, so make sure you shake the mixture before each use.

□□□□□□□□□□□□□□□□□□□□□□□□□□□□□□□□

Basic Cream Sauce

A nice heavy cream sauce can have two wonderful effects on you: first, it'll taste good and make you happy while you're eating it, and second, it'll sit so heavily in your stomach that you'll fall asleep right after dinner and get a good night's rest. The most popular kind of cream sauce served at Italian restaurants is Alfredo sauce, but a basic cream sauce can be combined with mushrooms, tomatoes, smoked ham, spinach, etc., etc., to make any number of delicious, solid sauces.

The one problem with making cream sauce is that to do it, you'll need some cream. If you happen to like cream in your coffee, you're in luck — you can use the same cream. If you don't usually have any cream in the house, you're going to need to go get some. Luckily, cream is the kind of thing often stocked at neighborhood grocery or convenience stores, so you might be able to pick some up without trekking all the way to your regular supermarket. If you do go out to get cream for a cream sauce, make sure that it's heavy cream; it will help give the sauce its thickness.

1. Start by bringing the cream to a boil in a pan or shallow pot, and then simmer it for a few minutes, maybe 5, while stirring.

2. Between stirring, cook some garlic in 1 tablespoon olive oil and/or melted butter in another pan.

3. Add the garlic/butter/oil to the cream, and at the same time add any herbs or spices you choose. Nutmeg, for instance, is a classic ingredient in Alfredo sauces. If you want a spicy cream sauce, you can use chili peppers or just basil and oregano.

4. When the cream has thickened to a consistency you like, you're done. It can take up to 1 hour.

If you're interested in making a classic Fettucine Alfredo, use the sauce with a lot of parmesan cheese to coat the pasta, but feel free to cut loose and add some fried mushrooms or cut up chunks of ham or steamed broccoli.

Try it with: Cream sauces work great with pasta, but also work with chicken and even, as a twist, as a burger topping.

Hummus

A long time ago, in a country far, far away, somebody invented hummus. If we had a few research assistants, we would be able to tell you where and when, but for now, it will have to suffice to say that this sauce or dip is really tasty and easy to make. It has a good amount of protein and not too much fat, so it's a good thing to snack on. Plus, it takes just about 5 minutes to make.

You'll just need:
chickpeas (also known as garbanzo beans, don't ask us why)
olive or vegetable oil
lemon juice

1. Get yourself a can of chickpeas (about 16-oz). Drain the water away, so you're just left with some chickpeas.

2. Mash the chickpeas until they're smooth.

3. Add 1 tablespoon lemon juice and 2 tablespoons oil, and about ½ teaspoon salt, according to taste. Mix it all up.

4. Garnish with some paprika, if you've got some.

Try it with: Bread, or on a sandwich with some vegetables and meat. We don't recommend putting this on your pasta, but you can try it if you want.

Recipes for 3 a.m.

Early to bed and early to rise makes a person healthy, wealthy, and wise — and clearly, college students are none of these things. The truth is that sleep is like a hobby for most college students: the kind of thing you do on the weekend and maybe one night a week, if you have a couple spare hours.

And while this book does not, in any way, intend to tell you that all-nighters are good for you or advisable, we do realize that they are, for many students, inevitable. But defeating your body's internal clock and tricking it into thinking that 4:22 a.m. is a nice time to be writing a history paper can be tough. One of your handiest tools in this deception is food and drink. If you can keep your body well-stocked with the essential fuels it needs for operation, it'll be that much easier for you to keep your eyelids open as you curse the rising sun and desperately widen the margins on your paper and increase the font size by 0.2%.

Below are several recipes that will keep you awake and satisfied on one of those long, lonely nights — which, of course, also apply to other late-night college experiences. No one said you had to be *working* until the sun comes up; students often find other excuses that prevent them from going to bed at a sensible hour. Either way, you'll need middle-of-the-night food, and here it is.

Some Spicy, Crunchy Stuff

It's a secret of truck drivers and air traffic controllers alike that if you're crunching on something with your teeth, it's harder to fall asleep. (Well, actually, no truck driver or air traffic controller was consulted to confirm this — but it makes sense, right?) So one of the best things you can make yourself to snack on in the wee hours of the morning is just a general mix of crunchy stuff. Some would call this cereal mix because cereal is often involved, but nuts, pretzels, crackers, and other such crunchy snacks work just as well. The basic idea is to make a coating that will spice up these snacks. After you bake it on, you can store the flavored mixture for up to a month in a sealed container, ready to be broken open when the occasion requires.

4 parts vegetable oil (but not much — say ¼ cup)
3 parts soy sauce
3 parts dried herbs and spices, whatever tastes good — chili, garlic, and onion powder to make it nice and spicy, with some oregano and basil thrown in
60 parts cereal/pretzel/cracker/nut mix

These are pretty approximate measures, if you couldn't tell.

1. All you've got to do is mix the oil, soy sauce, herbs, and spices, and then heat them up until they're hot.

2. Coat the cereal/pretzel/cracker/nut mix with the oil/sauce/herbs/spices mix and stir it all up until the former is coated with the latter.

3. Throw the whole thing in the oven on a low heat, around 275° Fahrenheit, and leave it in for 1 hour.

4. When it's done, take it out, let it cool, and then store it in an airtight container. Then the next time you're falling asleep at your desk between paragraphs of that oh-so-scintillating anthropology paper, take it out and crunch away.

Garlic Soup

One good way to make sure you stay awake is to make your breath reek so badly that it'll wake you up when you fall asleep. Seriously, though, a strong garlic soup will be warm enough to comfort you, as well as flavor-packed enough to jolt you to your senses without shocking your poor, debilitated 4 a.m. system.

Start with:

¾ cup garlic (this is a lot — this recipe is for *garlic* soup; use less if you'd like a less garlicky soup)
1 tablespoon onion
2 tablespoons olive oil

Fry these up together in the bottom of a big pot, big enough for the whole soup. Don't brown the onions and garlic, but just heat them up in the oil until they're soft. Then throw in:

¾ cup tomatoes (diced fresh ones or from a can)
1 quart stock
some pepper

After stirring it all together, simmer the whole thing for about 15 minutes. When you're done, you'll have a soup that will not only keep *you* up, but it'll also keep up anyone within twenty-five square feet of your breathing space.

Cookies

There are a number of factors that are generally supposed to motivate students to work hard and finish their assignments, even if it means staying up all night: good grades, parental and societal approval, higher potential wages, the respect of your peers (uh, *yeah*, right...), and of course, personal satisfaction. Except that none of these prove to motivate you like a warm batch of cookies. So, if you find your attention span lagging and your motivation to memorize the names and dates of forty-six British philosophers lacking, try baking a batch of these no-fail cookies.

1. First, beat the following together until they're light and fluffy:
   - 2 eggs
   - 1 cup butter or margarine (2 sticks)
   - 3/4 cup sugar
   - 3/4 cup brown sugar
   - 1 teaspoon vanilla

2. Then, mix these in their own bowl:
   - 2 1/4 cups flour
   - 1 teaspoon baking soda
   - 1/2 teaspoon salt

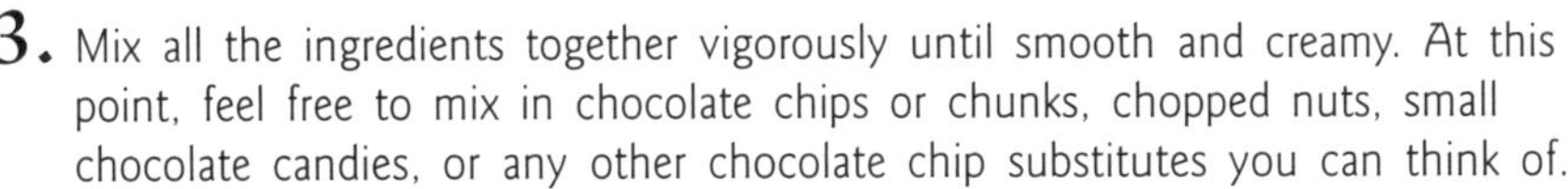

3. Mix all the ingredients together vigorously until smooth and creamy. At this point, feel free to mix in chocolate chips or chunks, chopped nuts, small chocolate candies, or any other chocolate chip substitutes you can think of.

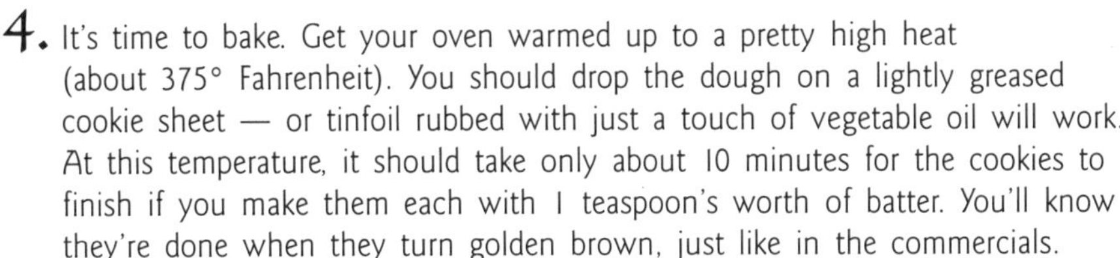

4. It's time to bake. Get your oven warmed up to a pretty high heat (about 375° Fahrenheit). You should drop the dough on a lightly greased cookie sheet — or tinfoil rubbed with just a touch of vegetable oil will work. At this temperature, it should take only about 10 minutes for the cookies to finish if you make them each with 1 teaspoon's worth of batter. You'll know they're done when they turn golden brown, just like in the commercials.

You'll get about 6 dozen cookies, enough to keep you eating until sunrise.

Brownies

Ah, chocolate. Scientists have already discovered that chocolate stimulates the same chemicals in our brains as certain illegal drugs do. No doubt in a few hundred years, chocolate will be banned and we'll look back on the chocolate-dependent society of the past with a mix of horror and pity, wondering how we could have allowed it to become socially acceptable to fixate on this strange but delicious drug.

But for now, you might as well eat as much of it as you can. One particularly effective delivery device for your needed chocolate fix — and those cravings come often in the wee hours of the morning — is a good, chewy, soft chocolate brownie.

You'll need:

6 ounces chocolate
½ cup hot water
4 egg whites
1 teaspoon vanilla
¾ cup sugar
¾ cup flour
1 teaspoon baking powder
a pinch of salt

1. Use the water to melt the chocolate in a bowl, adding the hot water slowly and stirring it until the chocolate is smoothly melted.

2. While the chocolate cools a bit, in another bowl, stir the sugar, flour, baking powder, and salt together.

3. Leave the dry ingredients for a second; whisk the egg whites and vanilla into the melted chocolate.

4. Stir in the dry ingredients.

You've now got your brownie batter. If you have a square cake pan, you should use it for baking the brownies, but otherwise you may have to improvise with a cookie tin — or you could just buy a cheap, disposable aluminum pan. The baking should take about 20-25 minutes on a heat of about 350° Fahrenheit.

And as the chocolate stimulates that illicit chemical in your brain, remember that it might not be legal for long. So eat up.

Caffeine and the All-Nighter

The sun is setting over your college campus. You've got sixteen physics problems to finish by 8 a.m. What's the usual college solution? Brew a pot of coffee, lock yourself in a room, and get cracking. (Well, that's after you call around unsuccessfully looking for someone who's already finished the assignment.) But before you further entrench your dependence on caffeine — a pretty serious, though widely consumed drug — you should at least be informed of its effects on your body, and how to use it most effectively.

As you probably know, coffee and many other drinks, such as tea and most soft drinks, contain caffeine. A 6-ounce cup of fresh-brewed black coffee contains about 100 milligrams of caffeine; a similarly sized cup of instant coffee contains about 65 mg; black tea, about 50 mg; soda, about 50 mg; iced tea, about 35 mg. Of course, the exact amounts of caffeine in any drink will depend on both the type of drink and how strongly it is brewed. And of course, the extent to which caffeine will affect you depends on your body size. A huge espresso shot might not make a 300-pound football player blink, while it'd make a 60-pound kid bounce off the walls until next Tuesday.

In general, though, for a regular-sized adult, the negative effects that we generally associate with coffee drinking — the shakes, a bad attitude, aches and pains, insomnia, etc. — result from a dose of caffeine of 200 mg or more.

Insomnia, though, is what you want, right? You want to keep your eyes open for that extra eleven hours. Unfortunately, experts say that while caffeine will keep you up, it won't keep your performance up to your regular awake standards. Also, here are some more scare tactics to keep you away from caffeine. It will dangerously raise your blood pressure, especially if combined with nicotine from cigarettes. It will possibly irritate any dry skin or other skin problems you've got. And like anything else in this world, it could possibly, in some unspecified way, cause cancer in you and birth defects in your baby if you're pregnant. Plus, once you're hooked, you'll experience withdrawal effects about twelve to sixteen hours after your last dose, physiologically nudging you to have more.

So if you can avoid coffee-fueled all-night study sessions, you should. It'll make you healthier, which will make it easier for you to get your work done and will make all-nighters less frequently necessary.

Having said that, if you're already a coffee-drinker, you're probably not going to stop now. That goes double if you like tea or caffeine-filled soft drinks, so we're not going to bother lecturing you any more about them. What we will do is offer some suggestions for spicing up your coffee and tea drinks — whether you use them responsibly is up to you.

Coffee

Brewing coffee is relatively simple, especially if you have a coffeemaker: two level teaspoons (flattened on top) for every six ounces of water, and let the machine do its work. Of course, if you don't have a coffeemaker you can just go the instant route. And the truth is, once you can brew coffee, you can add a lot to it to make it better. There is no particular recipe to follow, but according to your tastes, you might want to add any of the following: sugar, milk, cream, cinnamon, nutmeg, ice cream, chocolate syrup, honey, vanilla, chocolate powder (can be added to the coffee grounds before brewing, in the filter), or any of the other flavor essences you can buy at coffee shops.

If you want to make a coffee-flavored milkshake, remember that you needn't brew coffee first; you can just use instant coffee powder. About 2 teaspoons of coffee will make your vanilla milkshake that much more mocha.

Tea

As the coffee industry booms, the tea industry plays catch up, trying to find parallels to cappuccinos and iced mocha coffees for the non-coffee drinker. There are thousands of flavored teas on the market, ranging from cheap to very expensive. If there is a particular brand or flavor you prefer, go for it, but otherwise, realize that you can flavor your own tea easily. Of course, you can add any of the suggested coffee fixings on the previous page, or you can use tea's increased versatility to get a little more complex.

For instance, if you're a serious tea drinker, here's a recipe for chai tea — the spiced, creamy tea that has become very popular at teahouses. It involves a couple of "out-there" ingredients, but acts as a good example of the interesting twists you can put on your basic black tea.

To make 2 small cups of chai tea, the wacky spices you'll need are:

8 cardomom pods
8 whole cloves
1 inch-long cinnamon stick

These are weird things that even we don't really understand. You might not be able to find them at your neighborhood grocery, but if you go to a specialty, upscale market you should be okay.

1. In a pan, start heating 1½ cups water. Add the spices above and bring the water to a boil.
2. Lower the heat to a low heat, cover the top of the pan, and let it simmer for 10 minutes.
3. Add ⅔ cup milk and about 6 tablespoons sugar, and raise the heat just a bit so that it simmers again.
4. At this point, throw in 3 teaspoons regular, black, unflavored tea — you can use 3 regular teabags if you don't have any fresh tea — and turn off the heat and cover the pan again.
5. Wait another 2 minutes for the tea to soak in, then strain the mixture and serve. You'll get a sweet and spicy, creamy tea with a lot of Eastern charm.

Of course, that's a little complicated. You might just want to stick to straight-up teas with added fruit flavor or honey, or any spices you like. Remember that the less strongly you brew the tea, the less caffeine you're dealing with — so, if you can make your tea more dependent on added flavors and less dependent on actual tea, you'll have less of all those negative caffeine-related effects discussed earlier.

"Sure, I Eat like This *Every* Night": Cooking for Dates and Other Guests

You can admit it — there's no reason to be ashamed. Ninety-five percent of the reason you bought this book was so that you could cook well enough to impress a significant other or potential significant other, or potential one-night-long significant other. As the saying goes, the way to the heart is through the stomach. And you're certainly not getting *anywhere* with two-day-old frozen pizza. And you're probably also not going to do it with many of the basic recipes in this book. Those are for sustenance and survival — not style.

But for those *special* occasions, a little extra flair is necessary. Whether it's your second date with the cute redhead from bio lab or your parents have dropped in to see how their firstborn is doing at college, this chapter will give you the souped-up recipes to impress the pants off your dinner guests.

These recipes are different from those in the rest of the book in three ways. First, they may require you to do a dedicated shopping run to pick up a few special ingredients, which may in turn be more expensive than the stuff you already have on your shelves. In the recipes, we'll italicize these special ingredients so that you don't miss any of them. Second, they may involve more time-consuming or complex preparation techniques than the other recipes in the book (don't worry, you can still handle it.) We recommend that if the occasion is *truly* important — a one-year anniversary or something — you prepare the meal *twice*: one practice run in addition to the real deal. Third, each recipe is in two parts and the appetizers and entrées are specifically linked to each other to create full dinners. It's not that we don't trust the improvisational and creative skills that we've been trying to encourage in you throughout the other chapters, it's just that, well — OK, actually, we *don't* trust them. If you mess up a meal for yourself, it's no big deal. But if you mess up a meal for a potential significant other, we don't want that on our conscience.

We've given you recipes that are not only standouts, but will also create a complete dining experience that will be looked back on fondly by everyone involved. The recipes are scaled for two people, but feel free to make them bigger for larger special occasions such as parental and professorial visits or double dates. (See "'Anybody Got a Hairnet?'" on page 77 for hints on scaling recipes for larger groups.)

Before the recipes, here are a few general tips for making that dinner special:

Wine

First things first — we don't want any lawsuits. In America, at the time of printing, you have to be twenty-one to buy, serve, or drink alcohol legally. Also, anyone to whom you serve alcohol must be twenty-one. So if you're not or they're not, don't.

But if you do happen to be of age and you're hosting a special meal, you may want to purchase an appropriate wine to serve with the dinner you're cooking. While we could write a whole other book about the vocabulary and theory behind choosing the perfect wine, for now we'll just give you enough ground rules to get you started and make you sound a little bit less like the ignoramus that you are.

There are basically four kinds of wine on the market. White and red wines are the kind you should buy for dinner, rosé wines are good for picnics, and champagne is for marking a special occasion, but generally alone and not with food. If you plan to serve white wine with dinner, you should chill it in the fridge for a few hours before serving. Red wines are best served at room temperature. If you don't have a corkscrew lying around, buy one at the wine store for a couple bucks. Insert the corkscrew and loosen the cork a few minutes before your date or guests arrive, then open the bottle in front of them and make a big show of it.

Good wine comes from all over the world: France, California, Australia, Chile, wherever. So don't choose based on that. Choose based on price and on the appropriateness of the grape-type to the food you'll be serving. Traditionally, certain types of wine (defined by the type of grape used to make them, not where or when they were made) are matched with certain kinds of food. These are not hard and fast rules by any means, and you can mess around with them as much as you want. They'll just give you a guideline and make you seem like you know what you're doing.

The general idea in matching wine with food is to match the heartiness or fullness of the wine to the heartiness or fullness of the food. If you don't know what "hearty" or "full" wine is, don't worry — those are just words used to describe how strong the wine is. A full wine will have a lot of strong flavor, while a light wine will be less in-your-face. As a rule, white wines are lighter than red wines. So white wines are generally paired with lighter meals, like pasta, fish, and poultry, while red wines are paired with beef, pork, and other heavy meats. More specifically:

- For vegetarian dishes, light pastas, and light poultry and fish dinners, buy a Chardonnay or Sauvignon Blanc.
- For lighter meats like lamb, pork, some poultry, and heavy tomato-sauced

pastas, buy a Pinot Noir, Petit Syrah, or Merlot — these are medium red wines.

- Heavy meats, like beef and game meats, pair well with heavy Zinfandels, Syrahs, and Cabernets.

Probably the best way to choose a wine for dinner is to tell an overeager wine store employee what you're having for dinner; they seem to love to recommend wines, so you might as well let them have their fun.

Setting the Mood

We hope you've seen enough movies and TV shows to know the basics in this category — flowers on the table, candles, soft music playing (now's not a good time to listen to that new Dr. Dre disc), and a clean apartment. Burn some incense if you're into that sort of thing. Make sure you give the bathroom a good scrubbing so that your guests aren't horrified when they use it.

Appetizer: Roasted Beet and Arugula Salad with Goat Cheese

Entrée: Seared Sesame-Crusted Tuna with Whipped Purple Potatoes and Parsley Oil

First of all, realize how important it is to make sure that your date knows the *title* of the gourmet dinner you're preparing, and also realize that this evening is all about presentation. When you're out shopping for ingredients, think about how expensive it would be to take a date *out* to a dinner this nice, and cough up some bucks (though not close to as much) to make it happen at home.

Now, then, you'll need the following:

For the salad:

4 cups arugula (stemmed)
2 beets
½ cup toasted walnuts
1 teaspoon dijon mustard
12 tablespoons sherry vinegar
½ teaspoon sugar
1 tablespoon walnut oil
5 tablespoons olive oil
½ cup goat cheese
and of course, salt and pepper

1. Arugula is basically fancy lettuce, and it'll form the center of this salad. To start, you should wash and stem it (cut off the stuff that's not obviously leaves), and then cover it and set it aside.

2. Now you're going to set the beets roasting. Brush them with olive oil, salt, and pepper, and then cover them in tinfoil. You're going to want to roast them on a high heat in the oven, something close to 400° Fahrenheit, for 30-45 minutes. When you take the beets out, you need to remove the tinfoil, and then peel the beets. If you've roasted them thoroughly, the peel should slide right off with no problem. Cut the beets into thin slices and set them aside.

3. Toasting walnuts: no problem. Cook them in a pan on a low heat until they start to change color, just like toasted bread. Stir them around so that they don't burn.

4. To make the vinaigrette dressing, combine the mustard, vinegar, sugar, and salt and pepper and stir either in a blender or in a shakable jar, or just stir them hard. Add the oils slowly, bit by bit, while you mix them.

5. Now you're going to put it all together on nice plates and with some style. Toss the arugula in just a bit of the vinaigrette and lay it on a plate. Place some beet slices around the top — make sure they're nice and visible so that your guest can see how hard and complex this recipe is. Add some of the toasted walnuts to the top of the salad, and then sprinkle some goat cheese on. Drizzle the rest of the vinaigrette on the top and on the side of the salad, and serve.

For the entrée:

2 6-oz tuna filets
1 cup black and white sesame seeds
2 tablespoons olive oil
4 large purple or sweet potatoes
1 stick unsalted butter
½ cup heavy cream
2 cups Italian flat leaf parsley
1 teaspoon sugar
salt and pepper to taste
1 cup canola oil

1. First, make some parsley oil. (If you don't have a blender, you can't do this, so forget it.) To do this, boil the parsley in water for about 2 minutes so that

it's tender and then throw it in a bowl of ice water to "shock" it (stop the cooking process). Dry the parsley and blend it with sugar, salt, and pepper until it's smooth and then, as you blend, slowly add the canola oil bit by bit. Once you've added all the oil, blend for another 5 minutes. If you've got one, transfer the parsley oil into a squeeze bottle so that you can squeeze it onto the food later.

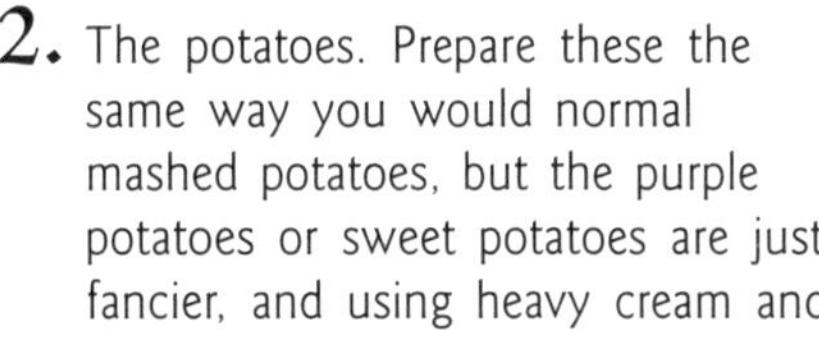

2. The potatoes. Prepare these the same way you would normal mashed potatoes, but the purple potatoes or sweet potatoes are just fancier, and using heavy cream and a lot of butter will make them very creamy. Boil the potatoes for about 15-20 minutes and then mash them with the salt, pepper, butter, and cream. We'd recommend that you *don't* add garlic if this is a date.

3. To make the tuna, pour out the sesame seeds on a flat surface or a plate. Season the fish with salt and pepper, and then lay the tuna flat on the seeds so that they stick to it. Then heat 2 tablespoons of olive oil in a pan until it's barely smoking. Cook the tuna seed-side down for about 2 minutes until a crust forms. Then cook the fish on the other side for 1-2 minutes, depending on how rare you like your tuna. Generally, people like tuna barely cooked at all.

4. When you've done all of the above, arrange the fish and potatoes stylishly. If you want to be trendy and do it like all the best restaurants, arrange the potatoes in a little lump in the center of the plate and cut the fish into 2 strips, and lay them diagonally on the plate so that they stick up in the air — as if you're building a tower of food, a monument of tuna and potatoes. Then squeeze on some parsley oil and use it to make the plate look pretty. Top the whole thing off with a little parsley.

This dinner, though it looks very complex, trendy, and fancy, is actually pretty easy to do. The cooking techniques are no different from those basic techniques that you've hopefully mastered: making sauces, mashing potatoes, frying fish. The difference here is in the ingredients, the combination of dishes, and the presentation. Hopefully, this difference will be enough to impress your guest.

Appetizer: Mussels in a White Wine* Tomato-Garlic Broth

Entrée: Penne in a Rosé Sauce with Roasted Tomatoes and Purple Basil

Mussels taste great and they are said to be an aphrodisiac — which means that, like Barry White albums and square-dancing, they get people in the mood for love. You might want to check in advance that your guest is willing to eat seafood, because some people have allergies or aversions to shellfish. In this menu, they're paired with a kicked-up, colorful pasta.

For the mussels:

1 pound mussels (New Zealand if available)
2 tablespoons olive oil
¾ cup chopped onions
1½ tablespoons minced garlic
½ cup dry white wine, optional
(*May substitute chicken or vegetable stock or broth for this item.)
6 Italian canned tomatoes (chopped)
5 tablespoons finely chopped flat leaf parsley
salt and pepper to taste

1. In a large sauté pan (basically, any big pan), heat the olive oil over medium heat. Add the mussels, sprinkle them with salt and pepper, and then cover the pan with a lid (or with another big pan or anything else you can find to use as a cover).

2. Let them cook for 3-5 minutes, then add onions, garlic, and stock or wine. Let them continue to cook for 1-2 more minutes, by which time the shells should have come open. Throw out any mussels that have not opened.

3. Add the tomatoes and cook until they're hot, then add 3½ tablespoons of parsley and remove the pan from the heat. Throw the whole mixture into a big bowl and add the rest of the parsley as garnish on top.

For the entrée:

4 tablespoons (extra virgin) olive oil
1 onion, diced
¼ to ½ a banana pepper, finely chopped, optional
2 garlic cloves, minced
2 large cans Italian tomatoes (strained and blended)
salt and pepper
2 tablespoons dried oregano
½ cup heavy cream
2 plum tomatoes
2 servings penne (measure on two plates for desired amount)

¼ cup purple basil chifonnade (rolled up basil leaves cut into strips)
¼ cup grated real parmesan cheese

To make the sauce:

1. Heat the olive oil in a saucepot (any small pot) over a medium-low heat.

2. Add the onions and cook them until they turn transparent. You don't want to let them color or turn brown. It should take about 15 minutes at this low heat.

3. Add the peppers and heat them until they get soft and tender.

4. Add the garlic and mix it around for about 1 minute — don't let it burn.

5. Turn the heat down to low. Then add the blended tomatoes and some salt, pepper, and oregano. Bring the mixture to a simmer.

6. Add the cream, enough to turn it to an orange-pink color, and then simmer the mixture for at least 1 hour, or until the sauce reaches a thick, rich consistency.

7. While the sauce is simmering, cut the plum tomatoes into 4 pieces each, sprinkle each with olive oil, salt, and pepper and place in the oven at about 400° Fahrenheit for 10 minutes. After 10 minutes, remove them from the oven.

For the pasta:

1. Make the pasta. (See "The Fundamentals" on page 40 if you don't know how to do this.) Basically, bring half a pot of water to a boil, add the pasta, stir it at first so that it doesn't stick, and then cook it for about 10 minutes until the noodles are as soft as you like them. Then use a strainer, colander, or the pot lid to separate the pasta from the water.

2. Heat up some olive oil in a pan on a medium-low heat. Add the sauce and the pasta and stir for 2 minutes. Place the pasta on 2 plates to serve, topping it with the roasted plum tomatoes, oregano, and basil. Add parmesan cheese at the table, like a waiter would.

And that's it. Once again, all you're really doing is making a basic pasta dish with a slightly complex sauce, and adding a simple, but exotic appetizer. Make sure to explain to your guest the difference, for instance, between the roasted plum tomatoes and the Italian tomatoes. And make up some weird story about mussels being an aphrodisiac — even if that's just a myth. It'll be sure to liven up the dinner conversation.

Appetizer: Roasted Red Pepper and Sun-Dried Tomato Soup

Entrée: Pan Sautéed Beef Tenderloin with Twice-Cooked Broccoli and Balsamic Reduction

Part of the task of preparing a high-class dinner is finding out what food your guests will and will not eat. This particular menu will do wonders for a carnivore, but won't score any extra points if your guest is a vegetarian. And you'll definitely be in trouble making the soup if you don't have a blender.

For the soup:

½ oz sun-dried tomatoes (don't use the oil-packed kind)
1 small onion
2 tablespoons olive oil
2 cups chicken stock
4 roasted red peppers — see "The Fundamentals" on page 47 for help with this
basil, chopped (use purple basil if you can find some; it's cooler)
salt and pepper to taste

1. We know it seems hypocritical, but you need to un-dry those sun-dried tomatoes — just soak them in water for about 1 hour.

2. Cook the onions in the biggest pan you've got, using the olive oil. Use a medium temperature and don't let the onions turn brown. It should take about 7 minutes.

3. Add the chicken stock, peppers, and tomatoes, as well as some salt and pepper, to the pan. Let this mixture simmer for 10-15 minutes.

4. Here's where the blender comes in. Pour the soup mixture into the blender and smooth it out for about 5 minutes or until it's nice and creamy.

5. Strain the soup to get rid of chunks, skin, and other undesirable elements.

6. Add herbs and spices to taste and serve it warm (which it should still be) with the basil as a garnish.

For the entrée:

2 8-oz filet mignon steaks
2 cups balsamic vinegar
1 bunch Chinese broccoli
4 tablespoons (extra virgin) olive oil
½ teaspoon crushed chili peppers
salt and pepper to taste

For the beef marinade:

¼ cup olive oil
2 tablespoons low-sodium soy sauce
2 garlic cloves
2 sprigs thyme
2 bay leaves

Mix all these things in a bowl and marinate the steaks in this mixture for at least 2 hours or overnight in the fridge. (Overnight will give you less to do on the day of the dinner, which will be good because you'll be plenty busy.)

To make the balsamic reduction:

In a small pot, simmer the balsamic vinegar until it reduces to a syrup, which should take about twenty minutes. Basically, all you're doing is heating up the vinegar so that the watery part of it evaporates and the part that doesn't evaporate becomes thicker and less watery. This isn't so easy, though, because if you burn the vinegar your whole kitchen will reek of vinegar for several hours. In the last five minutes of this reduction, you need to stir the vinegar and lift it off the heat now and again to make sure it doesn't burn.

To cook the broccoli the first time:

1. Wash the broccoli and cut about 1 inch off each stem.

2. Steam the broccoli. (See "The Fundamentals" on page 46 for help on doing this.) Basically, just set the broccoli in a strainer or colander over — but not touching — a pot of boiling water, so that the steam off the boiling water will cook the broccoli. Make sure you cover the top of the strainer. The steaming should take about 5 minutes to finish.

To cook the beef:

1. Remove the steaks from the marinade and scrape off the excess. By now, the flavor has seeped into the meat, so you don't need the juice on the outside.

2. Heat a couple tablespoons of olive oil in a pan over pretty high heat.

3. Sprinkle the steaks with salt and pepper and then place them in the pan.

4. Cook the steaks on each side for 1-2 minutes until a crust forms on the seared side.

5. Remove the steaks from the heat (lift up the pan) and lower the temperature to medium.

6. Now cook the steaks depending on how rare or well done you want them. 2-4 minutes will get them done rare, 3-5 for medium rare, and 4-6 or more for well-done.

7. When you're done cooking the steaks, take them off the heat and wrap them in aluminum foil. You want to let them sit wrapped in foil for at least 5 minutes (or up to 10) to allow their juices to settle.

Now, to cook the broccoli again:

1. Heat 2 tablespoons olive oil in a pan over a medium-high heat.

2. Add the broccoli and sprinkle it with salt and pepper. Then add the crushed chili peppers.

3. Toss the mixture for a couple minutes, but if the broccoli starts to turn brown or lose its bright green color, stop cooking it. Don't worry if the stalks turn a little brown, but you want the heads of the broccoli to look pleasantly green.

To present the whole thing real fancy and nice:

1. Remove the steaks from the foil, but keep the juices in the foil for later.

2. Cut the steaks in ½-inch thick strips and arrange them around the circumference of the plate (that's the outer ring, if you forget your geometry).

3. Put the broccoli in the middle and drizzle a little of the balsamic reduction over it. It doesn't take a lot; that stuff is strong.

4. Pour the steak juices on top of the meat and around the edges of the plate.

5. Whew. Done. Good job.

And it's as simple as that! (Actually, we know that it's not very simple at all, but that's the whole point of this chapter, right? And the truth is, you can make the balsamic reduction in advance and you can marinate the beef from the night before, so it's not so bad.)

Appetizer: Hearts of Romaine with Grilled Sweet Peppers in Garlic-Parmesan Dressing

Entrée: Citrus Marinated Chicken Breast with Herbed Potatoes and Fennel, Celeriac, and Bean Sprout Julienne

Here's a perfect example of how just a little more work — and most of that in the presentation department — can make the difference between the slop you throw together on your average Monday night and the five-star dinner that's going to make you a small celebrity to your date. Just dress up a simple salad-and-chicken dinner and give it a fancy name — it's easy to do, and it works.

For the salad:

2 hearts of romaine lettuce (get to the heart by peeling away the large outer leaves — what better metaphor for the romantic dinner you're preparing)
1 yellow pepper
1 red pepper
some olive oil
2 garlic cloves, minced
1 teaspoon red wine vinegar
1 tablespoon dijon mustard
2 tablespoons mayonnaise
juice of 1 lemon
salt and pepper to taste
2 anchovy filets from can, rinsed
½ cup parmesan cheese

First things first — make the dressing. Mix together garlic through salt and pepper until you get a creamy consistency. Put that aside.

To roast the peppers:

1. Coat the peppers in olive oil, sprinkle them with salt and pepper, and set them in the oven to roast.

2. Turn them every 3-4 minutes, and let them roast until they're almost completely black and charred on the outside.

3. Take them out and set them in a bowl and cover with plastic wrap. When they're cool enough to touch, cut them in half, pull off the charred peels, and remove the seeds from the center. Cut them into long, thin strips and set them aside.

To prepare the lettuce:

1. Cut the romaine hearts in half horizontally. Before proceeding, wash the lettuce — both the bottom halves and the lettuce leaves you cut off. You can either spin everything dry in a salad-spinner or dry the lettuce with paper towels.

2. Taking each of the bottom halves, carefully spread out the leaves in the shape of a flower bowl.

Final preparation:

1. Toss some of the lettuce leaves you cut off with the dressing.

2. Take that dressing-coated lettuce and put it in the lettuce bowls you made from the romaine heart bottoms. Layer the peppers and anchovy filets on top, drizzle on some dressing, and grate parmesan to top it all off.

For the entrée:

4 medium sized chicken breasts
1 celeriac (also known as celery root)
1 fennel stalk
2 cups bean sprouts
6-8 yukon gold potatoes
4 tablespoons olive oil
1 thyme sprig
1 tablespoon chopped parsley
1 rosemary branch
2 garlic cloves
salt and pepper to taste

For the marinade:

juice of two limes
juice of two lemons
juice of ½-1 orange
pepper
olive oil
2-4 garlic cloves, minced

For the vinaigrette:

juice of one lime
juice of one lemon
juice of ½ orange
¼ cup olive oil
salt and pepper

Also, get an empty can the size of a can of soup or corn. Wash it out and cut off the top and bottom and put it aside. You'll need it in a couple minutes to do some weird stuff.

Whew. Got all that? We'll try to make the instructions as concise as possible — you know, save paper and all that.

First:

Set the chicken marinating for an appropriate length of time. (If you need help with this, see the section on marinating in "The Fundamentals" chapter, page 50.)

For the julienne:

1. Just to explain what that word "julienne" means: it's a little salad made out of hard vegetables chopped in thin, matchstick-like slices. So, first things first: peel the celeriac and rinse it and the rest of the vegetables (the fennel and the bean sprouts). If the celeriac turns brown, rub it with a little lemon juice.

2. Cut the celeriac and the fennel into matchsticks.

3. Combine these in a bowl with the bean sprouts and set it all aside.

4. Mix the vinaigrette together, either by vigorously mixing or using a blender, and set that aside, too.

For the potatoes:

1. Scrub the outside of the potatoes to remove any dirt or weird growths.

2. Boil the potatoes in water for about 15 minutes, until they're tender when you poke them with a fork.

3. Immediately put the potatoes in a bowl of cold water and put them in the fridge.

4. After about 10 minutes, dry off the potatoes and cut them into small cubes. Heat up 2 tablespoons olive oil in a pan over medium-high heat.

5. Chop the thyme, parsley, and rosemary.

6. When the pan is hot, add the potatoes and sprinkle with salt and pepper. Cook them for about 4 minutes like this.

7. Then add the chopped garlic and cook for another minute.

8. Now add all the herbs, stir everything around, and remove the pan from the heat. Keep the whole thing warm, though. Leave it over a burner on the lowest possible heat or in the oven at the lowest possible heat.

To finish up:

1. Cook the chicken in a pan. Check "The Fundamentals," page 37, if you need help with this. It should take about 5 minutes on each side.

2. Toss the julienne with most of the vinaigrette.

3. Get a large platter or two individual plates. Put the hollow can you set aside (remember?) down in the middle of the platter/plates, and fill with potatoes. Slowly pull the can off, and you should be left with a tower of potatoes.

4. Lay the chicken on facing sides of the potato-tower, and the julienne on the other facing sides. Garnish the julienne with the rest of the vinaigrette and garnish the whole thing with any herbs you've got left.

Yeah, we know — for a fairly simple meal that seems like a lot of work. But the truth is, you'll feel like you've earned a relaxing evening, not to mention the respect of your date. And plus, you'll be too worn out from the cooking to be nervous.

"Anybody Got a Hairnet?": Cooking for a Crowd

It happens, sooner or later, in the life of every college chef: *They* descend on your apartment. *They* being the hordes, the great unwashed, the masses, the proletariat. Maybe it'll be the volleyball team, or the Model Congress kids, or just a bunch of hippies who want to listen to the new Phish CD — but they'll show up, squatting, sitting, and lying on every inch of free space in your apartment.

And, invariably, they'll be hungry. There are two ways to go as a host: the first is to announce to your guests that this little get-together is BYOE — AIYDTYP: Bring Your Own Everything — And If You Didn't, That's *Your* Problem. Of course, while such an approach will save you time and effort, it won't win you any popularity contests or get you elected student body president. And depending on the temperament of the group, you might find yourself under siege as they, like locusts, systematically wipe out all your supplies. Your other choice is to graciously welcome your guests into your home, make sure they're comfortable, and then get cracking on making some food so that they don't revolt.

In this chapter are a bunch of recipes that can be cooked as snack food for big groups, as well as tips on how to make bigger batches of recipes in other sections of the book. Of course, big parties are going to blow out your ingredient supply no matter what happens — and that's going to cost you money — so you might want to throw a limit on how many of these bashes you have per week. Or, if your place has somehow become a designated hanging-out zone, you may want to ask people to chip in either ingredients or cash to fund the food supply.

Meal Multiplication

If you think about it really hard, probably the easiest way to make food for a lot of people is to make the same kind of food you'd make for yourself, and just make a whole lot more of it. To do this, all you need to do is employ the good old times table and multiply out the quantities of ingredients in your favorite recipes.

Do not make the mistake of multiplying cooking times. As long as you have a large enough cooking surface to handle your larger batch, the food should cook at the same rate as usual. One exception to this is that boiling larger pots of water on the same-sized stovetop or with the same immersion heater will take longer. This makes sense, because the same amount of heat has to do more work.

Use the conversion table on the last page of this book if you're having trouble converting between teaspoons, tablespoons, quarts, pints, etc.

If you're making big batches of food, you may be able to skimp a little on expensive ingredients. For instance, often a little bit of herbs will go a long way. Also, if you're out shopping for a big party, you may as well buy prechopped vegetables or preshredded cheese if they're not too expensive, because they'll save you valuable time when it comes down to preparing the recipes.

Of course, the best advice we can give you if you're planning to cook for many people is to start early and make more than you think you'll need. That way, if something messes up, you won't have to order pizza — or if you do, there'll be time for it to arrive.

Nachos & Salsa

Ever since salsa became the number one condiment in America, nachos have been in the spotlight. But just because there are seventy-six brands of premade salsas at the supermarket and as many kinds of nacho chips doesn't mean that the nachos you serve have to be boring and predictable. By all means, buy tortilla chips in the store, but if you find yourself without them and with a gang of guests, remember that you can also make tasty homemade chips by frying little bits of tortilla in a little oil. As for premade salsa — unless you like wasting your money on an inferior product, you might as well make your own.

See the Classic Tomato Sauce recipe on page 51 for help with making your own salsa. Basically, though, salsa is a lot easier to make than pasta sauce because you don't need to warm it up or cook it. You just need to cut up small chunks of tomato, cucumber, and onion and add chunks of chili peppers, fruit, corn, or other vegetables as you like. Throw in lots of herbs (oregano, basil, chives, cilantro, whatever) to make the flavor a little more complex.

Once you've got a solid, spicy salsa and some good nacho chips, make sure you don't just toss these out to the crowd. Spread out the chips on a baking sheet, cookie tray, or around the edges of a large bowl, cover them with shredded cheese, fried ground beef, and sliced vegetables. Heat in an oven or microwave until the cheese melts. Dole out sour cream and more salsa in small bowls, as well as some guacamole if you've got it.

Speaking of guacamole, here's how to make some. You're going to need avocados, obviously, but once you've got those, you can probably improvise with the regular ingredients you keep in your kitchen. Remember that guacamole is just a specific kind of vegetable dip and the specificity is just that avocados are the basic ingredient, so there are no real rules about what else you have to put in. Some recipes recommend sweetening your guacamole with fruits, such as peaches or guavas, or spicing it up with cilantro. And don't let us stop you — but for now, here's a recipe that you can whip up in no time:

Basic Guacamole

2 avocados
1 garlic clove
1 tomato
1 onion
1 tsp lime juice (if you have it)

There are a couple things you need to do before you start mashing and mixing this up into a proper, creamy guacamole texture. Make sure that the avocados are ripe — they should be soft and pliable, not rock-hard — and then skin them and take out their pits. And, of course, chop up the tomato, garlic, and onion.

Cook for Crowds

Fried, Battered Anything

Admit it. You'd eat a shopping cart if it were deep-fried and battered. That's because fried stuff tastes *good*. And fried snacks are some of the easiest snacks to make. So next time you have a lot of people over, do this:

1. Get a pan over some high heat and get it nice and oily; the entire bottom of the pan should be covered in oil.
2. Crumble up a bunch of bread, crackers, or plain cereal in a bowl until you have a sand-like crumb mixture. Add some salt, pepper, or spices.
3. Crack an egg into a bowl and stir it up until it's uniform.

4. Grab anything — mushrooms, peppers, onion chunks, hot dog bits, boiled potato chunks, carrot slices, whatever. Dip them in the egg, roll them around in the breadcrumbs until they're coated, and then throw them in the pan until they're fried golden brown.

Serve these fried things with ketchup, mustard, and maybe some homemade dip (see below).

▽△

Dip Recipes

The theory here is that something that tastes vaguely good will taste better when you cover it in something else that has more flavor. That makes the creation of dips very liberating because you can add absolutely anything you want to, so long as you think it'll make whatever you're eating taste better. This applies to potato chips, chopped vegetables, and battered anything. Here are a couple of quick ideas for basic dips you can make with basic ingredients. The truth is, most of these dips are so simple that you'll probably be annoyed that there are even recipes for them. But you should try them out anyway — if nothing else, they'll get you started experimenting with your own dips.

Mustard Dip

The simplest possible mustard dip is just mustard. But if you don't want to look like a slacker, you can spice up your mustard with a few classic dip ingredients. Take:

3 parts mustard — for this dip, thicker Dijon mustard is better
4 parts vinegar
2 parts honey
4 parts olive oil

Combine them in that order. At the end, add some chopped fresh herbs. Dill would complement the Dijon taste very well. And remember that you can vary the proportions according to what you'd prefer in a dip; if you like it sweet, up the honey content; if you like the mustard taste, use more of that.

Cream Cheese Dip

If you need a dip on the spot, all you have to do is sacrifice a package of cream cheese from your fridge. You'll need to thin it out, which you can do by mixing it in a bowl with milk until it reaches a thin, dippy consistency. Then you can add flavor: salt, pepper, garlic, chopped onions, lemon juice, Worcestershire sauce, soy sauce, cheddar cheese, whatever.

Sour Cream Dip

Sorry, but this is basically the same as the cream cheese dip above, except that it tastes more like sour cream than it does like cream cheese. Actually, it's even easier because sour cream is already at a good dip consistency. Just add some chopped onions or onion powder (or if you have some onion soup mix, that'll work nicely), garlic, chopped vegetables, ketchup, or anything else you can think of.

Sweet and Hot Dip

Got an apple? Got a chili pepper? Good. Now go get some green onions and a lemon, and you can make this exotic-tasting dip. You'll need:

- 1 medium-sized apple, grated in a cheese grater or cut into small pieces
- 1 tablespoon chopped chili peppers
- 2 tablespoons brown sugar (or you can sub honey, if that's easier)
- 1 tablespoon grated lemon peel
- 2 tablespoons lemon juice
- 2 tablespoons chopped green onions (also known as scallions)

Mix everything but the onions until you get a smooth mixture. Then stir in most of the onions and sprinkle the rest on top. You'll be surprised by the taste of this one, but who knows? You might like it.

Cook for Crowds

Pigs-in-a-Blanket

People get married for many different reasons, but more than one groom in the history of the world has gotten married just so that he could have as many pigs-in-a-blanket as he wanted at his wedding. For some reason, the thought of these mini, crispy hot dog things is enough to make men get over their lifelong fear of commitment. But just imagine if you could serve up a tray *whenever you wanted*. You might never have to get married at all.

The amazing thing is that making pigs-in-a-blanket is simple. You just need some dough and some hot dogs.

To make the dough:

If you're really lazy, just buy some premade, expensive pastry stuff from the supermarket. If you're willing to put in just a little work, you can make your own dough, like this:

1. Melt 8 tablespoons butter.
2. Blend it (or mix it vigorously by hand) with 4½ ounces of cream cheese.

3. Stir in 1 cup flour.

4. Let the mixture sit in the freezer for about an hour, until it's nice and firm.

To make the hot dogs:

If they're precooked hot dogs (and most are) then all you need to do is let them thaw out or defrost them in the microwave if they're frozen. Then just cut them up in little slices, maybe 1 inch in length.

Then:

Take the dough out of the freezer, break off a thimbleful of it, and wrap it around a piece of hot dog. Lay the little uncooked piggies on a baking sheet and bake them on a high heat, around 450° Fahrenheit, until they turn brown, which should take about 15 minutes. Serve them with mustard and ketchup, and think about a new reason to get married as you toss them, one by one, into your mouth.

Punch

While we do not encourage the use (and especially the excessive use) of alcoholic beverages, we do know that there are some people in college who drink alcohol. Those people, we hope, are all legally allowed to, being twenty-one years old and possessing legal identification which proves that fact. When some of those people get together in big groups, they sometimes consume fairly large amounts of alcohol. It is more convenient for the host of those people — who is also certainly twenty-one years old with identification to prove it — to make a large alcoholic concoction, often referred to as a punch, rather than making many individual alcoholic beverages.

Of course, you can always make big punches without liquor. Here's a simple punch recipe that you should try out and experiment with:

- 2 packages powdered soft drink mix or other fruit juice powder, whatever flavor you like
- 1 bottle vodka (in the 750-1000 ml range)
- 1 bottle fruit juice — say, orange or apple or whatever
- 1 bottle cheap red wine

Perhaps you noticed that these specifications weren't exactly, well, exact. The truth is that as long as it tastes sugary and fruity, and as long as there's enough liquor in there to keep your guests happy, any punch is fine. You might want to try adding some sherbet and mixing it around until it melts, or putting in some chunks of fresh or canned fruit. And since cold punch is almost always better than warm punch, you should also probably throw in some ice.

Account Balance: $00.15: Eating on a Tight Budget

College is an expensive proposition. First you've got to pay for TV, then cable, then clothes, movies, weekend road trips, spring break in Cancun, CDs, posters, video games, a pool table, and oh yeah, tuition and books. With all that, it's not surprising that sometimes the college student's cash flow flows decidedly in the direction of *broke*. Every once in a while — end of the semester, when a big phone bill comes due, just after that fateful night at the casino — you may find yourself in a dire economic situation, with not a lot of money to throw around on luxuries like "food."

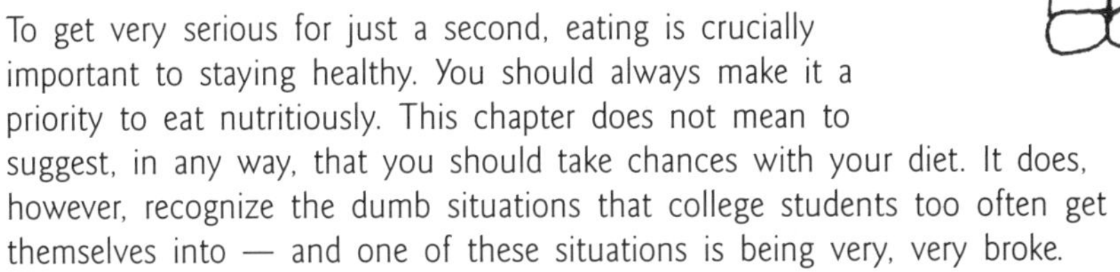

To get very serious for just a second, eating is crucially important to staying healthy. You should always make it a priority to eat nutritiously. This chapter does not mean to suggest, in any way, that you should take chances with your diet. It does, however, recognize the dumb situations that college students too often get themselves into — and one of these situations is being very, very broke.

With that in mind, this chapter has a series of suggestions on how to absolutely maximize your food budget. Following the suggestions in this chapter will not lead to particularly tasty eating. However, if you've ever found yourself in the position of needing to eat very cheaply or if you're the type of person for whom the gross mismanagement of finances is a work of art, you may at one point or another need some of the information below. Good luck — and next time save your money and save yourself the trouble.

Free Food

The cheapest kind of food is free food, and when your budget is close to non-existent, just a little free food can go a long way. There are a few ground rules that this book has to set for your quest for free food. No stealing (we're not going to support it, though it's certainly effective — there's always food in jail) and no lying or fraudulently begging (i.e., if you're not deaf and blind, don't say you are just to get a bite of somebody's burger — that's just immoral). But you'd be surprised how often an honest request can score you some free grub.

For instance, any restaurants or fast food places that prepare fresh food in advance usually have to chuck out all the leftovers at closing time. This includes bagel shops and donut shops, as well as regular bakeries, where the products are baked in large batches and there are almost always some leftovers. Even pizza places have to do *something* with their leftover slices at closing time. Plus restaurants often have to get rid of fresh produce that they haven't used by the end of the night. If you're in the right place at the right time — and the right time is the last possible moments of closing time, when the employees are just cleaning up and getting ready to head home — and you ask politely, you may get lucky. Some restaurant employees are obviously going to be nicer than others; some may be college students themselves and will empathize with your plight. Others may fear losing their jobs (it's general official company policy, especially at franchises of large fast-food chains, *not* to hand out leftovers), or some might just be jerks. In any case, if you ask politely, you haven't done anything wrong, and the worst they can do is say no. In the best case scenario, you'll walk home with a sweet bag full of donuts or bagels that will remain edible, especially if kept in the fridge, for at least a couple of days.

Another untapped source of free food ingredients is at restaurants. Often, restaurants give out free supplies to accompany their meals — and as long as you don't make off with an entire knapsack full of sugar packets, you're not really stealing. (Well, this is a gray area. But again, if you ask politely, most restaurants won't care at all if you grab a couple extra butter packages for the road.) The kinds of things you should never have to pay for when your budget has hit rock bottom are sugar, salt, pepper, butter, jam, tea, ketchup, mustard, barbecue sauce, vinegar, maple syrup, and even olive oil. Just bring small bottles if you plan on making off with liquid, and don't overstep your bounds, or you'll risk persecution and prosecution. A five-star luxury restaurant is probably not the best place to pick up free groceries while wearing a tank top, shorts, and flip-flops. And it's not smart to attempt to make off with a basket of dinner rolls no matter what kind of restaurant you're at.

When making your rounds for freebies, make sure not to forget large supermarkets where free samples are often given out. If there's someone giving out cubes of sample cheese, you might be able to persuade them into giving you two, four, or ten more than usual. Not only will you work on your public speaking and leadership management skills, but you'll already be on your way to a free sandwich.

Cheap Food Sources

It's true that the best things in life are free; the second-best things in life are generally very, very cheap. If you've zeroed out your bank account, you're going to need to take advantage of these cheapest sources of food in your area to make it through your moments of financial difficulty. There will inevitably be some inconvenience involved on your part in obtaining super-cheap food, but that's the price you pay for being broke. One general rule: avoid all brand names like the plague. Someone you've never heard of makes it cheaper every time.

The first option to look into is what's called a discount or warehouse supermarket. These are chains or individually owned supermarkets that eschew all the frills of your everyday, luxurious supermarket to give you the very best possible price. So you'll have to bag your own groceries and the layout may not be all bright and cheery as you're used to, but you can't eat bright and cheery supermarket layout, can you? Look in the Yellow Pages or on the Internet to find chain or warehouse stores. Typically in a store like this, you can save 25% or more off retail supermarket prices. Every little bit helps, right?

Even if you can't get to a discount supermarket, you can still cut a good deal off the price of the major expensive items on your shopping list, such as bread and meat. Sad as it seems, you can do this by buying *old*. Two or more day-old bread, baked goods, and meat that are just about to pass the expiration date are g-*old* in your search for low-cost nourishment. Slightly older bread and meat could go for 40% less than its fresh rivals — or even cheaper.

When buying old baked goods, check thoroughly before purchase for any mold spots; if there's none or just an isolated outbreak, you'll probably be fine, but if you buy an entirely mold covered loaf of bread, no matter how cheap it is, you're wasting your money. Vacuum-packed baked goods or those in sealed plastic containers are the best to buy old, and usually large supermarkets will have a small section of their bakery department devoted to these day-or-two-old items.

When you get old baked goods home and you want to eat them, heat them up first. The warmth will make them more palatable and will trick you into thinking they're at least related to their freshly baked rivals. Old bread works much better as toast than it does in non-toasted form, in which case it's dried out anyway by the toasting. And as you know from Mary Poppins, just a spoonful of sugar makes the medicine go down, so lather on the toppings (to the extent that you can afford them or get them for free) and make your crusty bread go down. As long as the bread isn't moldy, it won't hurt you, no matter how dried out it is.

The process of using old meat is similar. Make sure the meat you buy isn't *way* past its sell-by date (usually stores will start reducing meat prices on the last day of recommended sale). Also, check the cut of meat itself for visible signs of rotting, discoloration, bad smell, or disfigured shape. Buying rancid meat cheap is like paying a lot for a stomach infection, so make sure you save money, but also get safe meat. If the supermarket is selling the meat to you on the last day of recommended sale, then that means the meat is safe to eat or freeze that day. You should definitely not leave it in the fridge for a couple days. But if it's cooked or frozen on the last day of recommended sale, you can consider it 100% safe.

In general, if you have to hesitate, you should probably hold off. There's always ways to eat cheaply on a vegetarian budget. That said, if you do buy some old meat, heat it up real hot when you get it home. Cook it a *lot*. Just as boiling water kills the bacteria floating around in it, heating meat up very hot can kill a lot of the germs that may or may not be lurking inside. Old steak is not a good time to indulge your taste for rare meat; you want it well-done, completely well-done. Again, if the cut of meat isn't the best, use a lot of affordable toppings to make it more palatable.

Like shopping in general, the pursuit of old food is a treasure hunt. Sometimes you'll come back empty handed and sometimes you'll discover the mother lode. Like anything else, if you don't have money, you're going to need to spend a lot of time. So hit more than one supermarket if you can, and dig through those day-old-bread baskets looking for the best loaf. With a little luck, you'll find something decent.

And, of course — make your grandmother proud and use coupons. If grocery store fliers don't get delivered to your apartment, grab one as soon as you get to the supermarket and study it thoroughly before you start making your way through the store.

Cheap Recipes

Once you've found whatever free and unusually cheap food sources you can, you now have to splurge on retail-price ingredients to fill in the gaps in your pantry. At this point, you want to buy the cheapest staple foods which will fill you up with no frills like "flavor": eggs, beans, rice, and pasta. Get a lot; if you stuff yourself with these energy-rich foods to the point of almost passing out, then you won't be able to waste money on snacks. As for vegetables and fruit: corn, beans, and broccoli are often cheapest, as are bananas. And if you're truly broke, you should just be drinking tap water, but if you feel the need for some flavored beverage, go for powdered juice crystals.

Below are a couple of meal suggestions that just involve cheap staple foods and the condiments that you can easily acquire for free from restaurants. The truth is, though, that almost every recipe in this book can be made on a microscopic budget, if you shop wisely and waste nothing. So these are just a few examples. Leaf through the other chapters and you'll find that you'll be able to get a lot further on a couple of bucks than you thought you could.

Bean Chili

Canned and dried beans are much cheaper than meat, but contain similar amounts of protein with less fat. In other words, if you like the taste of beans, you should eat them a lot as a substitute for meats for health and budget reasons. However, if you don't like beans (and you'd be in the majority) you should still eat them, especially when your budget is struggling.

Canned beans are pretty cheap, and they're easy to cook, too. All you have to do is warm them up, really. You can make a good vegetarian chili by frying onions, peppers, and whatever vegetables you like in a pan and then adding some canned kidney beans and tomato sauce (or just ketchup or diced tomatoes) and chili powder. You can add a can of corn as well, if you can afford it. Fried ground beef will add quite a bit of taste (you should fry this up first, or separately, and then add it to the chili near the end), but of course, if you could afford beef, you probably wouldn't be messing around with beans, anyway. Add water to your chili if you like it with a thinner texture or just leave it if you like it thick and chunky.

Serve a vegetarian chili over some boiled rice and you've got a substantial, hearty meal.

Frittata

"Frittata" is basically a fancy word for omelet; maybe it's fancy enough to convince you that what you're eating is somehow heartier than just a quick breakfast dish. Actually, you can make a frittata seem more substantial than a standard omelet in a couple ways. First, you can fry it up a bit and then bake it in a really shallow pan so that it forms a crust and starts to resemble an egg-cake. Second, you can add weighty chunks of boiled potato and steamed broccoli to your frittata to make each bite pack a nutrient-and-energy punch.

To make a big lunch frittata, you'll just need:

1 potato
a couple spears of broccoli
3 eggs

If you've got some cheese kicking around, go ahead and add it, too. But if all you've got are the three things above, you're still in good shape.

1. Start by boiling the potato and steaming the broccoli (according to the directions on page 46).

2. Stir the eggs up in a bowl (add milk, if you can afford any, and salt and pepper) and then fry the eggs in a pan as you would scrambled eggs until they begin to solidify.

3. Then, in a really shallow pan, baking tin, or a plate with a substantial rim, mix the eggs with smaller-than-bite-sized chunks of vegetables.

4. Set the whole thing to bake for about 15 minutes on a high temperature, around 450° Fahrenheit, until a crust has formed on top.

5. Remove from the oven, let it cool off, and eat it straight from the baking pan if you like.

If you're eating this for breakfast, you're allowed to call it a baked omelet. But if your financial situation has forced you to eat this for lunch or dinner and you want to feel like it's a foreign delicacy and not just a fancy breakfast, make sure to call it a frittata.

French Toast

The most classic diet for those suffering cash flow problems is bread and water, of course. French toast is just slightly better, being made of bread, water, and eggs. You're welcome to soup up your French toast with vanilla extract, white or brown sugar, milk, crushed walnuts, or whatever — but right now, you're probably struggling to afford just the bread. The good news is that even bread that's a little stale (so long as it's not moldy and disgusting) will work fine for this cheap breakfast-and-brunch recipe. So:

1. Crack some eggs in a bowl, about 2 eggs for every 3 standard-sized slices of bread. Mix up the eggs and add milk if you've got some (about 1 tablespoon of milk per egg). If you don't have milk, you can just add a little water, a bit less than 1 tablespoon of water per egg. Add sugar, about 2 teaspoons' worth per egg, if you've got it. A pinch of vanilla or cinnamon couldn't hurt either.

2. Now heat up a pan on a high frying heat and coat it in a little butter or oil.

3. Dunk your bread pieces in the egg mixture until they're entirely coated. Then fry them up on both sides until the egg mixture solidifies and the toast turns golden brown.

Serve with some cleverly obtained free maple syrup or with nothing, if that's what you've got. It's basically bread and water (and eggs) — but it tastes good.

The Morning After

While the author and publisher do not encourage the use (or excessive use) of alcoholic beverages, we are aware that consumption to excess, with the inevitable hangover, does occur from time to time. The only real cure for the hangover is moderation or abstinence in the first place. Failing that, we offer the following suggestions that might be of some help.

College is about gaining experience, right? And experience is about making mistakes, right? So, when you were slow dancing with the lamppost at dawn yesterday, wearing just your boxers and a towel over your shoulders like a cape, that was a good thing, right?

Well, have no fear. We're not here to judge you, but to comfort you and make you feel better. Truth be told, we've all been there before, and we feel your pain — that throbbing headache, the nausea, the unexplained nakedness.

It's ironic for a cookbook to tell you this, but the best idea — at least at first — might be not to eat anything for a little while. If your stomach is truly queasy, you'd be better off just giving it some time to recover. But if you do get hungry soon and you feel like trying to swallow something, then we've got some inoffensive recipes that we hope will go down without too much trouble. (They'd also probably be handy if you're truly ill, so keep this chapter in mind when your nausea isn't just self-inflicted.) And, like it or not, there's a section below that's going to explain to you how to avoid this problem next time.

I Told You So... (The Night Before the Morning After)

Despite their intense familiarity with the substance, an astonishingly small percentage of college students truly understand how alcohol works in their bodies and why it often hurts them.

Most college students do understand that a major part of hangovers — and the adverse effects of alcohol in general — stems partly from dehydration. As your body tries to process, break down, and generally rid itself of the socially acceptable poison we call alcohol, it uses an incredible amount of water. It needs this water to dissolve the alcohol, and if it can't get that water from your stomach, it will take it from your blood, lymph, and brain. And that is not good.

The solution is relatively simple — drink water. Guzzle a glass of water between alcoholic drinks at parties and gun down a couple glasses of water before you go to bed. Morning after time — if you feel too queasy to choke down water or juice, try leaving some ginger ale or lemon-lime soda out to get flat and giving that a go. (There's one exception to this "Hydrate, hydrate, hydrate" rule — if someone has become ill to the point of vomiting, doctors advise you not to encourage them to drink water. They'll just throw it up, and it'll further irritate their esophagus.) If you're just having a few drinks, though, drinking water or a water-and-electrolyte sport drink before, during, and after will help, though it won't do the whole job.

There's a much less widely known cause of hangovers and general drinking malaise: congeners. Congeners are toxic byproducts of the alcohol distillation process, and give different alcohols different colors and tastes. Their toxic properties are the source of those throbbing hangover headaches that make you feel like there's a guy jack-hammering directly against your brain.

Because congeners are inevitably going to be in the alcohol you drink, there's not much you can do to fight them except choose drinks that are less congener-heavy. Generally, the darker the liquor, the more congeners it has. Hard-core, old-man drinks like scotch, brandy, and worst of all, bourbon, have up to thirty times the congeners of lighter, transparent drinks like gin and vodka. Same goes for red wine, which has more congeners than white. And, unfortunately, that's what the high price tags of expensive liquors often connote. For instance, the distilling process, so often touted by high-class brands of vodka, does remove impurities including congeners and makes the liquor easier for your body to process.

Another way to reduce the harm that congeners can cause you is to avoid mixing different types of drinks. This is another piece of wisdom generally accepted throughout college society, but the reason why you shouldn't chase a tequila shot with a gin and tonic and then a scotch on the rocks is that it quite literally confuses your body. Your liver and kidneys are all set to go to work on some tequila, when all of a sudden they need to change gears and tactics to tackle the gin, and then again when the scotch shows up. So pick a drink and stick with it.

And, as an aside, a stern caution: absolutely, positively do not take aspirin, Tylenol, or any similar drug after you've been drinking. You also really shouldn't take anything like this for an entire day before you plan to drink because it'll mess you up in strange and dangerous ways. Taking these drugs after drinking can result in internal bleeding, release of serious toxins in your digestive system, and worse. Don't mess around with this. If you need to, take these drugs the morning after when you're knee-deep in your hangover, but do not try to skip the sleeping/sobering-up step and just take the aspirin right away.

Going to bed drunk — as wonderfully tempting as it is — is a bad idea. Your body, when it's awake and functioning, is pretty good at getting rid of the alcohol inside it. When you go to sleep, you turn off many of your internal repair crews and the alcohol is not dealt with nearly as effectively. Every hour you can stay awake while you're still feeling drunk is another hour of effective hangover prevention.

Of course, the simplest way to ensure that you don't feel sick the morning after is to exercise a bit of caution and judgment the night before. Know your tolerance. (And don't say, "How can I know my tolerance without testing its limits?" That's just dumb.) And relax about it — you shouldn't be out there to impress anybody by drinking a ton, but to have a good time — and a good time involves you feeling healthy and good.

▽△▽△▽△▽△▽△▽△▽△▽△▽△▽△▽△▽△▽△▽△▽△▽△▽△▽△

The Classic "Remedies"

There are a few classic foods to eat when you're nauseous. Some may be effective for medical reasons, some may be placebos, and some may make things much worse. With that in mind, you can give them a shot and see what works for you.

One nausea remedy sworn to by many experienced hangover fighters is flat ginger ale or lemon-lime soda. Open a bottle, let it sit for half an hour or so, and then try forcing that down. It may be easier than even water and some say it'll settle your stomach. Another such remedy is burnt toast — maybe the theory is that the stomach doesn't want normal food, but it'll settle for food that is in about as good a condition as it is. So toast up a piece of bread until it starts turning black, cut off a little piece and try that.

Some heavy drinkers will claim that the only *real* cure for a hangover is some "hair of the dog that bit you" — in other words, a little bit of whatever it was you were drinking the night before that got you into this mess in the first place. Now, adherents of this method aren't completely crazy; a little alcohol in the morning will ease the pain (even if it's the pain of too much alcohol) just as a little alcohol made you feel good, at first, the night before. But "hair of the dog" just delays the inevitable symptoms of a hangover and is probably not a good idea.

Another mysterious traditional remedy with no sensible scientific explanation is lemon juice under the armpits. We'll forgive you if you decide not to bother trying that one.

You probably don't feel like eating anything yet, but if your stomach is settling down, you'll start to get hungry soon. Often, you won't start to feel better until you've eaten something. By all means, eat whatever food will be most comforting to you in this weakened state — if you're the type that goes for pickled herring or greasy pineapple pizza, that's cool. But we'd like to suggest a couple of non-confrontational dishes that won't upset you with too much flavor or spice.

Mashed Potatoes

Mashed potatoes are one of the most basic, minimalist foods. Devoid of color and form, they are food in the abstract, and you can make them taste like just about anything, or like nothing. If your stomach is still doing cartwheels to rival the Olympic Gymnastics team, you might want to stick to basic, light mashed potatoes that'll give you some energy and revive you without upsetting your stomach.

1. You'll need a potato or two. Peel them if you like or leave the skin on if you prefer — but do cut them up into quarters. Boil the potatoes in salted water until they're tender. This should take about 15-20 minutes.

2. Get the potatoes out of the water and into a pan. (Use a fork or just drain the water out of the pot and then plop the potatoes into the pan.) Put the pan over a low heat and mash the potatoes up with a couple of forks. Add about 1 teaspoon milk per potato (or if your stomach can't handle milk, just plain water) to help soften them up and make the mashing easier. Add salt and pepper and any other flavors — garlic, for instance, if your stomach is up for it — as you mash.

Potato Soup

Once again, potato-the-wonder-food comes to the rescue. This potato soup is thick and creamy, not too bland, but just bland enough for your current condition.

You'll need:

6 parts potato
1 part onions
a little butter, milk, and flour

1. Chop up some onions and potatoes into little pieces. You should use about 6 times as much potato as onion — say, 1/4 cup onions, and 1½ cups potatoes. Combine these and cover them in a saucepan with water and then heat the mixture until it boils. Simmer it for about 10 minutes, until they're soft. Drain the water.
2. Melt 1 teaspoon butter in a pan. Then add 1½ cups milk and 1 tablespoon flour. Stir it around until it's smooth and heat the mixture gently to thicken it.
3. Add the potatoes and onions to the milk mixture and heat it up nice and hot, and then eat it.

Chicken Soup

"Urban legend" is one way of phrasing it. "Traditional knowledge" is another. Either way, grandmothers agree that chicken soup cures all ills — even hangovers. And while you could buy some instant chicken soup powder or some condensed chicken soup in a can, nothing would make your grandmother prouder than if you developed your very own unique chicken soup blend. So, here it is:

1 teaspoon vegetable or olive oil
1/4 cup each: onions, carrots, and celery
1 cup potatoes, peeled and diced
1½ cups chicken stock (canned, or chicken bouillon cubes or powder mixed with boiling water)
½ cup milk
1/4 cup noodles or pasta
½ teaspoon garlic powder

1. In the biggest pan you've got — and it better be really big — or in a pot if necessary, fry up some onions, carrots, and celery in a little bit of oil over a medium heat. Cook them for about 5 minutes, until the onions are tender.

2. Add the potatoes and chicken stock. Cover the top of the pan and let it cook for about 20 minutes.

3. Add the milk, noodles, and garlic powder and simmer for another 10 minutes, until the noodles are soft. If you have some leftover cooked chicken, you can chop it up and throw it in at this point, as well.

The cool thing about this soup is that almost every part of it is optional. If you don't particularly want onions, carrots, and celery, you don't have to have them, and you can just lop off the whole first step of the recipe. If you don't want potatoes in there, you can ignore that, too. You will need to keep in the chicken stock and the milk, and you'll probably want to at least have some noodles in there. Even the simplest chicken soup possible still has the grandmother-tested healing properties that you seek. So make yourself a mug of soup, curl up on the couch with it and the remote control, and just wait until you start feeling better.

Further Research

By now, you've been through this book cover to cover, and you've mastered it all. You can make hash browns in your sleep, cook a five-star meal without batting an eye. Balancing your budget is easy, and you eat as nutritiously as, well, a nutritionist. And maybe that's good enough for you. On the other hand, you might have liked a few of the things you learned here. Maybe you felt empowered by your ability to make phenomenal scrambled eggs. Perhaps you'd like to take your cooking to the next level.

No problem. Below you'll find a list of resources that will guide you through the next steps of your culinary journey. Most of these books and websites are easy to find and use, maybe not *quite* as easily as this book, but by now you're ready for a challenge.

So, go out into the world and cook. Good luck. And remember, if you can eat it, you can cook it. Probably.

Recipes

Nowadays, you can get thousands of recipes with just a few clicks. Most of the sites listed below have quick search engines to help you find what you need.

You can search for recipes and buy that new stainless steel broccoli strainer you've been dreaming about at www.cooking.com.

Check out *SOAR — the Searchable Online Archive of Recipes*. You'll find recipes, recipes, and a couple more recipes at www.recipesource.com.

Meals for You at www.mealsforyou.com not only lets you find recipes, but will aid you in designing entire week-long menus — with shopping lists, too.

The Recipe Archive (www.cs.cmu.edu/~ mjw/recipes) is an archive of recipes.

Culinary Schools

If you think you're really a lost cause in the kitchen, you can always spend a few weeks, months, or years paying an expert to instruct you in the culinary arts. Many of these schools offer general programs and some offer instruction in a particular field — sushi, French cooking, or other specializations.

One of the world's most respected and extensive cooking schools, Le Cordon Bleu, has programs in Paris, London, Hawaii, and a number of other exotic locations. They offer quick summer programs in addition to professional training, and they're just snooty enough to satisfy even the most picky wannabe gourmet. You can find information on all their programs at their website, www.cordonbleu.net. Another cooking school of interest is The Culinary Institute of America in Hyde Park, New York. For more information visit their website, www.ciachef.edu. Or look into the cooking school program of the Johnson & Wales University in North Miami, Florida, at www.jwu.edu/florida.

If you're interested in a kind of cooking not covered in this book at all — because we have no idea how to do it — you could always study at The California Sushi Academy. They offer three-month programs that will qualify you as an assistant sushi chef, and they'll help you find a job rolling up raw fish in seaweed. Look into it at www.sushi-academy.com.

If you're vaguely interested in attending a cooking class or school program but have no idea what kind or where, check out http://cookforfun.shawguides.com. This exhaustive site lists thousands of culinary programs, trips, academies, one-time lectures, and other culinary-education-related information, organized and searchable by geography, topic, and more.

Nutritional Resources

You may — for good reason — question the nutritional benefits and detriments of eating like a college student. Seventeen straight days of pizza is not exactly the diet recommended by professional nutritionists. There are a number of excellent websites that will analyze your diet, tell you what you need more of and what you need less of, as well as offer nutrition tips and suggestions. For free.

The first place you should surf to for nutritional information is a U.S. government site that has collected a number of resources on one page. From there, you'll be able to find whatever you need. The site is www.nal.usda.gov/fnic/etext/000108.html. We suggest you bookmark it so that you don't need to type *that* in every time you want to find out how many calories there are in a hot dog.

Let Us Know What You Think

We welcome any feedback or comments you'd like to share about this book, the recipes, or just about anything else. Contact the publisher (who will in turn contact Josh) at editorial@spsstudios.com.

Recipe Index

Conversion Table

1 gallon	=	4 quarts	=	3.8 liters
1 quart	=	2 pints	=	950 milliliters
1 pint	=	2 cups	=	470 milliliters
1 cup	=	16 tablespoons	=	240 milliliters
1 tablespoon	=	3 teaspoons	=	15 milliliters
1 teaspoon	=	2 half-teaspoons	=	5 milliliters